IMPACT
SOCIAL STUDIES

U.S. History
Making a New Nation

INQUIRY JOURNAL

Mc
Graw
Hill

Program Authors

James Banks, Ph.D.
University of Washington
Seattle, Washington

Kevin P. Colleary, Ed.D.
Fordham University
New York, New York

William Deverell, Ph.D.
University of Southern California
Los Angeles, California

Daniel Lewis, Ph.D.
The Huntington Library
Los Angeles, California

Elizabeth Logan Ph.D., J.D.
USC Institute on California and the West
Los Angeles, California

Walter C. Parker, Ph.D.
University of Washington
Seattle, Washington

Emily M. Schell, Ed.D.
San Diego State University
San Diego, California

mheducation.com/prek-12

Send all inquiries to:
McGraw Hill
120 S. Riverside Plaza, Suite 1200
Chicago, IL 60606

ISBN: 978-0-07-691409-8
MHID: 0-07-691409-7

Printed in the United States of America.

8 9 10 11 LWI 25 24 23 22 21

D

Program Consultants

Tahira DuPree Chase, Ed.D.
Greenburgh Central School District
Hartsdale, New York

Jana Echevarria, Ph.D.
California State University
Long Beach, California

Douglas Fisher, Ph.D.
San Diego State University
San Diego, California

Nafees Khan, Ph.D.
Clemson University
Clemson, South Carolina

Jay McTighe
McTighe & Associates Consulting
Columbia, Maryland

Carlos Ulloa, Ed.D.
Escondido Union School District
Escondido, California

Rebecca Valbuena, M.Ed.
Glendora Unified School District
Glendora, California

Program Reviewers

Gary Clayton, Ph.D.
Northern Kentucky University
Highland Heights, Kentucky

Lorri Glover, Ph.D.
Saint Louis University
St. Louis, Missouri

Thomas Herman, Ph.D.
San Diego State University
San Diego, California

Clifford Trafzer, Ph.D.
University of California
Riverside, California

Letter From the Authors

Dear Social Studies Detective,

Think about the United States of America. Why did different groups of people decide to settle in the territory that would become the United States? When the nation was formed, how did the economy, the politics, and groups of people change? In this book, you will find out more about how a territory became a nation. You will think about what it meant to become an independent United States—and what it means to be an American.

As you read, take on the role of a detective. As questions come to your mind, write them down. Then analyze the text to find the answers. What grabs your interest? Take notes as you read. You will use your notes as you share what you learned with your classmates. Look closely at all of the text—photos, maps, time lines, and historical documents will bring the history of the United States to life!

Enjoy your investigation into the world of social studies where you will explore how a group of territories became the United States, a place full of women, men, and children who came from many places to form a growing and diverse country!

Sincerely,

The IMPACT Social Studies Authors

The Declaration of Independence

Contents

Reference Source

Chapter 1

The Land and Native Peoples of North America

How Were the Lives of Native Peoples Influenced by Where They Lived?

Chapter 2

The Age of Exploration

ESSENTIAL EQ QUESTION

What Happened When Diverse Cultures Crossed Paths?

Chapter 3

A Changing Continent

ESSENTIAL EQ QUESTION

What Is the Impact of People Settling in a New Place?

Chapter 4

The Road to War

 Why Would a Nation Want to Become Independent?

Chapter 5

The American Revolution

 What Does the Revolutionary Era Tell Us About Our Nation Today?

Chapter 6

Forming a New Government

 How Does the Constitution Help Us Understand What It Means to Be an American?

A Growing Nation

What Do the Early Years of the United States Reveal About the Character of the Nation?

Chapter 8

The Civil War

 EQ ESSENTIAL QUESTION **What Was the Effect of the Civil War on U.S. Society?**

Skills and Features

Inquiry and Analysis Skills

Reader's Theater

My Notes

Getting Started

You have two social studies books that you will use together to explore and analyze important Social Studies issues.

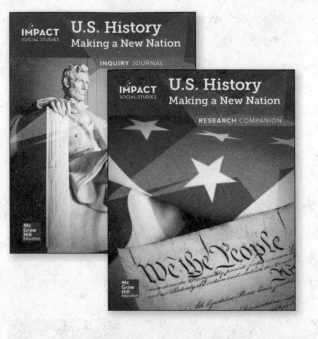

The Inquiry Journal

is your reporter's notebook where you will ask questions, analyze sources, and record information.

The Research Companion

is where you'll read nonfiction and literature selections, examine primary source materials, and look for answers to your questions.

Every Chapter

Chapter opener pages help you see the big picture. Each chapter begins with an **Essential Question**. This **EQ** guides research and inquiry.

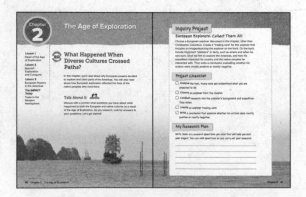

In the **Inquiry Journal,** you'll talk about the **EQ** and find out about the EQ Inquiry Project for the chapter.

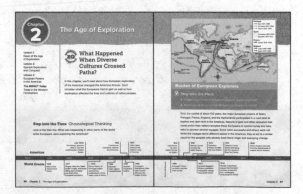

In the **Research Companion**, you'll explore the **EQ** and use a time line and map to establish the lesson's time and place.

Explore Words

Find out what you know about the chapter's academic and domain-specific vocabulary.

Connect Through Literature

Explore the chapter topic through fiction, informational text, and poetry.

People You Should Know

Learn about the lives of people who have made an impact in history.

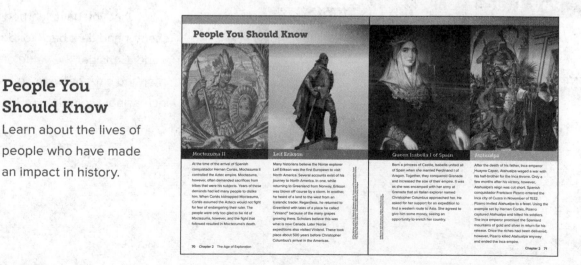

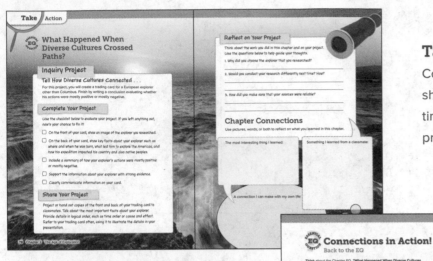

Take Action

Complete your Inquiry Project and share it with your class. Then take time to discuss and reflect on your project. What did you learn?

Connections in Action

Think about the people, places, and events you read about in the chapter. Discuss with a partner how this gives you a deeper understanding of the EQ.

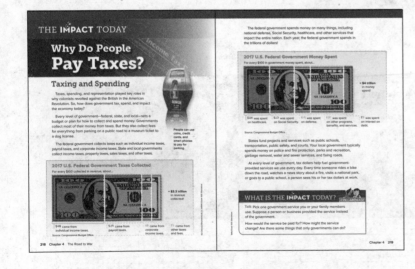

The IMPACT Today

Take what you have learned in the chapter and tie it back to today's world. Consider the value of informed citizenship to an increasingly complex world.

Every Lesson

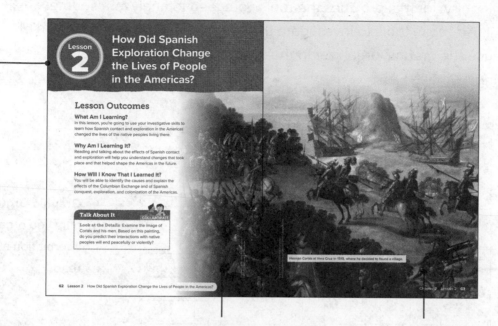

Lesson Question lets you think about how the lesson connects to the chapter EQ.

Lesson Outcomes help you to think about what you will be learning and how it applies to the EQ.

Images and text provide opportunities to explore the lesson topic.

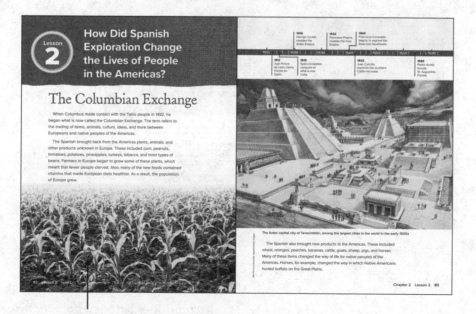

Lesson selections deepen your understanding of the lesson topic and its connection to the EQ.

Analyze and Inquire

The Inquiry Journal provides the tools you need to analyze a source. You'll use those tools to investigate the texts in the Research Companion and use the graphic organizer in the Inquiry Journal to organize your findings.

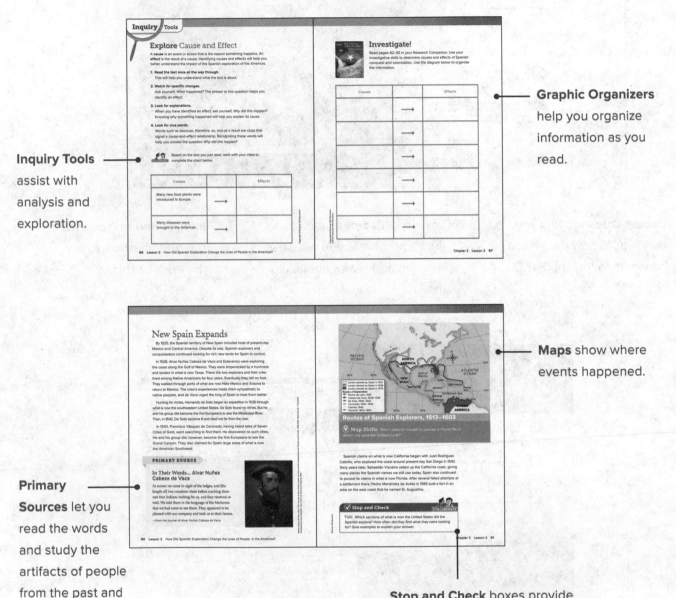

Inquiry Tools assist with analysis and exploration.

Graphic Organizers help you organize information as you read.

Primary Sources let you read the words and study the artifacts of people from the past and present.

Maps show where events happened.

Stop and Check boxes provide opportunities for self-assessment, to consider different perspectives, and to make connections.

Report Your Findings

At the end of each lesson, you have an opportunity in the Inquiry Journal to report your findings and connect back to the EQ. In the Research Companion, you'll reconsider the lesson focus question based on what you've learned.

Think about what you have learned.

Write About It using text evidence to support your ideas.

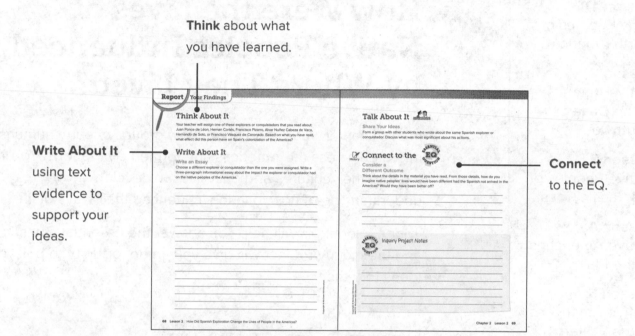

Connect to the EQ.

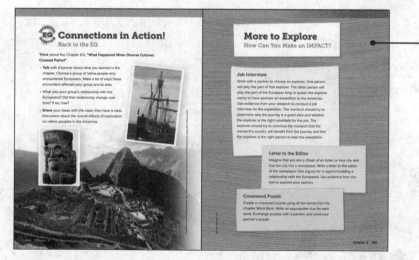

Think about what you read in the lesson. How does this give you a new understanding about the lesson focus question?

Chapter 1

The Land and Native Peoples of North America

ESSENTIAL EQ QUESTION

How Were the Lives of Native Peoples Influenced by Where They Lived?

In this chapter, you'll read about how groups of early humans migrated across the Americas and formed civilizations. You'll explore their cultures and daily lives to develop an understanding of how location influenced their ways of life.

Your explorations will help you answer the Essential Question, and the Inquiry Project will give you an opportunity to pull your ideas together.

Talk About It COLLABORATE

With a partner, discuss who you think lived in the Americas before the arrival of the Europeans and what their lives might have been like. As you read and research, look for answers to any questions you have. Let's get started!

Inquiry Project

Show What Life Was Like . . .

A museum has asked you to design a display for a Native American group that you'll study in this chapter. Create a poster or diorama to showcase an aspect of this group's daily life before the 1500s. You might focus on the group's tools, clothing, or shelter, or you might depict the group's spiritual or cultural traditions, government, or economy. Think about how location and surroundings affected the group's daily life. Prepare a museum plaque to describe your visual.

Project Checklist

- ☐ **Choose** a Native American group from the chapter that you'd like to research.

- ☐ **Decide** on an aspect of the group's daily life or culture that you'd like to explore.

- ☐ **Research** and gather information from reliable sources.

- ☐ **Create** a museum display to communicate the information you found in your research.

- ☐ **Make** a plaque for your museum display.

My Research Plan

Write down any research questions you have that will help you plan your project. You can add questions as you carry out your research.

_____

_____

_____

_____

_____

Explore Words

Complete this chapter's Word Rater. Write notes as you learn more about each word.

endeavor

My Notes

- ☐ Know It!
- ☐ Heard It!
- ☐ Don't Know It!

_____

_____

_____

harvest

My Notes

- ☐ Know It!
- ☐ Heard It!
- ☐ Don't Know It!

_____

_____

_____

hieroglyph

My Notes

- ☐ Know It!
- ☐ Heard It!
- ☐ Don't Know It!

_____

_____

_____

hunter-gatherer

My Notes

- ☐ Know It!
- ☐ Heard It!
- ☐ Don't Know It!

_____

_____

_____

mesa

My Notes

- ☐ Know It!
- ☐ Heard It!
- ☐ Don't Know It!

_____

_____

_____

oral history

My Notes

☐ Know It!
☐ Heard It!
☐ Don't Know It!

_____
_____
_____

potlatch

My Notes

☐ Know It!
☐ Heard It!
☐ Don't Know It!

_____
_____
_____

prairie

My Notes

☐ Know It!
☐ Heard It!
☐ Don't Know It!

_____
_____
_____

slash-and-burn

My Notes

☐ Know It!
☐ Heard It!
☐ Don't Know It!

_____
_____
_____

totem pole

My Notes

☐ Know It!
☐ Heard It!
☐ Don't Know It!

_____
_____
_____

How Did the Characteristics of Early Native American Groups Develop?

Lesson Outcomes

What Am I Learning?
In this lesson, you're going to use your investigative skills to examine how early Native American groups living in different regions developed special characteristics.

Why Am I Learning It?
Reading and talking about these early Native American groups will help you understand how the regions in which they lived affected the development of their special characteristics.

How Will I Know That I Learned It?
You will be able to analyze information to identify the characteristics of early Native American groups, give an opinion about how their surroundings influenced the development of these characteristics, and support your opinion with evidence.

Talk About It

COLLABORATE

Look at the Details The ancient structure in this image was built between 800 A.D. and 900 A.D. What do you think this structure was used for?

The Kukulkan pyramid in Mexico was built by the Maya people.

1 Inspect

Look Read the caption below the map. What do you think the term "land bridge" means?

- **Circle** words on the map that identify land areas and bodies of water.
- **Trace** possible migration routes followed by early humans.
- **Discuss** with a partner how the last Ice Age caused early humans to migrate into North America.

My Notes

_____

_____

_____

_____

_____

_____

_____

_____

_____

_____

_____

Early Humans in North America

Many major ice ages have taken place in Earth's history. During these periods, sheets of ice thousands of feet thick covered vast areas of land. With so much seawater trapped in ice sheets, or *glaciers*, sea levels dropped. Dry land appeared in some places. During the last major Ice Age, from about 30,000 to 12,000 years ago, sea levels dropped very low. One theory is that a land bridge formed between the northeast tip of Asia and the northwest tip of North America. Scientists refer to this area as the Bering Land Bridge, or *Beringia*. Herds of Ice Age animals moved from Asia to North America across Beringia, looking for food. Many scientists think that early humans from Asia followed the animals they hunted across this land bridge.

Sometimes a hunting trip could take many days. The hunters had to gather plants to eat until they were able to kill an animal. The plants they gathered included berries, grasses, and mushrooms. This is why we call these people hunter-gatherers.

Scientists think that humans first reached North America sometime between 30,000 and 12,000 years ago. Once in North America, these early humans may have migrated southward on land. Another possibility is that they avoided the ice by traveling in boats along the Pacific Coast.

ARCTIC OCEAN

B E R I N G I A

SIBERIA

ALASKA

Bering Sea

The Bering Land Bridge, or Beringia, linked Asia and North America during the last Ice Age.

PACIFIC OCEAN

2 Find Evidence

Look Again Underline words in the text that explain how the spread of glaciers during the last Ice Age caused Beringia to develop.

Examine Look back at the map. How does the map show the outline of Beringia? How does it show the outline of current landmasses?

3 Make Connections

Talk Using the symbols on the map, discuss with a partner the types of Ice Age animals that early human hunters followed into North America. What does this tell you about the hunting skills of these early humans?

Analyze Information

To analyze information means to break the information down into parts and then look at how those parts fit together. Analyzing information will help you determine what the information means and how it will be useful.

1. **Read the text once all the way through.**

   This will give you a general idea of the subject, what kind of information is available, and how it might fit together.

2. **Look closely at the sources of information.**

   Do you trust that source will provide accurate information?

3. **Ask questions about what you are reading.**

   Questions such as *who, what, where, when*, and *why* can help you break the information down into parts.

4. **Note important patterns, relationships, and trends.**

   Taking note of important information in a graphic organizer can help you better interpret information.

COLLABORATE

Based on what you have just read about Beringia, work with your class to complete the chart below.

Location	Surroundings	Way of Life
Beringia and North America during the last Ice Age		

Investigate!

Read pages 10–19 in your Research Companion. Use your investigative skills to find information in the maps, images, and text that will help you understand one early Native American group from a geographic area mentioned in the lesson. Use the chart to organize information.

Location	Surroundings	Way of Life

Think About It

Based on your research, how do you think the location and surroundings of the Native American group you picked affected the way the people lived?

Write About It

Take a Stand

Write and Cite Evidence Write a brief, three-paragraph informational essay describing how the location and surroundings of the Native American group you chose influenced the way the people lived.

_____

_____

_____

_____

_____

_____

_____

_____

_____

_____

_____

_____

_____

_____

_____

_____

_____

Talk About It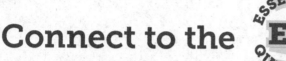

Compare Your Groups

Talk to a classmate who chose a different Native American group. What was similar about the ways your two groups lived? What was different?

Geography

Connect to the

Pull It Together

Think about the people you have learned about in this lesson. How did location and surroundings affect the way early Native American groups lived?

_____

_____

_____

_____

_____

 Inquiry Project Notes

_____

_____

_____

_____

_____

_____

_____

How Did the People of the Desert Southwest Meet Their Needs?

Lesson Outcomes

What Am I Learning?

In this lesson, you're going to use your investigative skills to learn about the cultures of the Pueblo, Navajo, and Apache peoples.

Why Am I Learning It?

Reading and talking about how people live in harsh desert conditions will help you understand how people adapt to their environment.

How Will I Know That I Learned It?

You will be able to compare and contrast different groups of Southwestern Native Americans and explain how they lived in the desert.

Talk About It

COLLABORATE

Look at the Details Look closely at the picture. What meaning or purpose do you think these markings may have?

Petroglyphs at Peñasco Blanco ruins

Navajo Ceremonies

1 Inspect

Read Study the translation of the Navajo song "Jó Ashílá." Then read the description of Navajo Ceremonies.

- **Discuss** with a partner why songs and ceremonies like "Jó Ashílá" and Enemyway are important to people.

- **Think** about special occasions when people might sing a song.

My Notes

_____

_____

_____

_____

_____

_____

_____

_____

_____

_____

_____

_____

There are more than sixty major Navajo ceremonies. These are religious ceremonies that can last more than a week. These ceremonies may contain more than five hundred songs. The ceremonies are long and complex and are led by highly respected singers. Dancers in masks help represent various spirits in the ceremonies. Sand paintings, designs using brightly colored sands, are made specifically for each ceremony.

The Enemyway is a week-long ceremony meant to bring balance to people's lives. This ceremony was originally performed for warriors coming home from battle to help them return to everyday life. Today, it is also performed as a healing ceremony for people who are ill. "Jó Ashílá" is a song performed as part of the Enemyway ceremony.

Jó Ashílá

Hee yėe' yaa' a', hee yėe' yaa' a', Jó a-shí-lá,

jó a-shí-lá, jó a- shí-lá, hee yėe' yaa' a',

T'óó-gá ni-zhó-ní-go baa hó-zhó lá, hee ya hėe hee yá,

Jó a-shí-lá, jó a-shí-lá, jó a-shí-lá,

Hee yėe' yaa' ya', T'óó-gá ni-zhó-ní-go

łįį' gá N-dáá gi béézh ní'-áázh lá, hee ya hėe hee ya',

T'óó-gá ni-zhó-ní-go N-dáá gi łįį' gá béézh ní'-áázh lá,

hee ya hėe hee ya', Jó a-shí-lá, jó a-shí-lá,

jó a-shí-lá, hee yėe' ya wėi yaa' ya'.

Here is the English translation of "Jó Ashílá."

Traveling together, happy about beauty. It is beautiful that they both came on a horse at the Enemyway.

Special items used in an Enemyway ceremony

2 Find Evidence

Reread What is the song "Jó Ashilá" about? Circle words that help support this.

Examine Are the lyrics of the song meant to be taken exactly as it says? What else could this song mean? Why do you think this?

3 Make Connections

Talk Why do the Navajo perform these rituals?

Explore Compare and Contrast

To **compare** is to find the similarities between two things. To **contrast** is to find their differences.

Similarities and differences can be linked. Two cultures may have similarities because they both came from the same group or they both live in similar environments. A difference in cultures, however, could mean that one group has an advantage or hardship that the other group does not.

To compare and contrast:

1. Read the text all the way through.

This will help you understand what the text is about.

2. Look for keywords related to the information you want.

If you are looking for information about housing, look for words like *house*, *home*, and *build*, or materials like *wood* and *stone*.

3. Summarize the information.

Make quick, simple answers to your questions.

4. Review your answers.

Ask yourself, "*Which are the same?*" "*Which are different?*" "*Why?*"

Based on the text you just read, work with your class to complete the chart below comparing rituals and ceremonies.

	People in Your Community	Navajo
Rituals and Ceremonies		

Investigate!

Read pages 20–27 in your Research Companion. Use your investigative skills to look for text evidence that tells you about the lifestyles of different Native American groups of the Southwest. Then, think about what is similar and what is different and why.

	Pueblo	Navajo	Apache
Housing			
Culture/Religion			
Economy			

Think About It

Review your research. Based on the information you have gathered, how did native peoples live in the deserts of the American Southwest?

Write About It

Write from a Different Perspective

Write a diary entry from the viewpoint of a Pueblo, Navajo, or Apache person. Be sure to include details about where you live, what you eat, what chores or jobs you do, and what possessions you have.

_____

_____

_____

_____

_____

_____

_____

_____

_____

_____

_____

_____

_____

_____

Talk About It

COLLABORATE

Discuss

In small groups, consider what you have learned about the Native Americans of the Southwest. How have they adapted to life in the desert?

History

Connect to the

ESSENTIAL EQ QUESTION

Pull It Together

Think about what you have learned about the Native Americans of the desert Southwest. What traditions continue to be used today? Why have these traditions continued?

_____

_____

_____

_____

_____

_____

ESSENTIAL EQ QUESTION Inquiry Project Notes

_____

_____

_____

_____

_____

_____

_____

How Were Native Peoples of the Pacific Coast Shaped by Their Surroundings?

Lesson Outcomes

What Am I Learning?

In this lesson, you're going to use your investigative skills to find out how different groups of Native Americans were affected by their surrounding environments.

Why Am I Learning It?

Reading and talking about the geographic features of California, the Pacific Northwest, and the Arctic and Subarctic will help you understand the differences in the cultures of the Native Americans who lived there.

How Will I Know That I Learned It?

You will be able to identify the relationship between where a group of people lived and the customs and practices of its culture.

Talk About It

COLLABORATE

Look at the Details What do the people at the back of the boat do? What do the rest of the people do? Look for evidence that this is a ceremonial hunt.

Native Americans used to hunt from canoes along the Pacific Coast.

1 Inspect

Look Examine the image of a totem pole.

- **Circle** the figures depicted on the pole.
- **Discuss** with a partner what order the totems appear in and what they might represent.

My Notes

_____

_____

_____

_____

_____

_____

_____

_____

_____

_____

_____

_____

_____

_____

_____

"Ridicule" totems, often used to shame individuals, appear upside down.

Totem Poles

The images carved on totem poles are often human, animal, or spiritual forms that represent something important to a family. For example, some Native Americans have used wolves, eagles, and grizzly bears as symbols for their families. Totem poles have also been carved in honor of an important person or event. Today, these structures are associated with Native Americans across the Pacific Northwest, but they originated with groups in southeastern Alaska such as the Tlingit and the Tsimshian.

Totem poles vary in height, but most are 10–50 feet tall. They can be placed in front of a family's home or beside a gravesite. Shorter ones may be kept inside the home. Totem pole carving nearly died out in the late 1800s when the U.S. government banned a number of Native American ceremonies. Native Americans revived the practice in the 1950s and continue to make totem poles today.

Totem-pole carvers usually make the poles from the wood of red cedar trees. Before a tree is cut down, native peoples may hold a ceremony of respect and thanks for the use of the tree.

On a pole the top totem, called a crest, often shows which clan the family belongs to. An upside-down totem is sometimes included to make fun of an enemy. Most totems have oval shapes. The carver may use colors or patterns in the wood to help determine designs.

2 Find Evidence

Infer What type of story might this totem pole tell? How do the totems and their order help tell that story?

Think Where would you place this totem pole in a village so that its message would be best delivered?

3 Make Connections

Talk Look again at the totem pole on the previous page. Think about the qualities or history of your family or an important person to you. Create an object, drawing, or other way to represent your family or this important person. How is your way similar to or different from the totem poles used by some Native American groups?

Explore Compare and Contrast

You can better understand the ideas in a text if you **compare and contrast** the details the author provides.

1. **Read the text.**

    This will help you understand what the text is about.

2. **Think about how the text is organized.**

    If the text is divided into sections that each focus on a place or a group of people, look for topics that the author mentions in every section— for example, housing and customs. The author may be expecting you to draw comparisons.

3. **Reread and look for text features.**

    Authors often use text features when they want to call attention to the similarities and differences between ideas. Analyze text features, looking at headings, bulleted texts, and images.

4. **Make notes in a chart.**

    You can use these notes later to help you remember what you read.

With the class, work to fill in one circle of the Venn diagram on page 27 using information about the Tlingit people from the previous page.

Investigate!

Read pages 28–35 in your Research Companion. Use your investigative skills to compare the Tlingit people with two other Native American groups from this lesson. Consider where each group lived, its customs, and its artifacts. Use the Venn diagram to show things that are unique to and common among the different groups.

Tlingit People

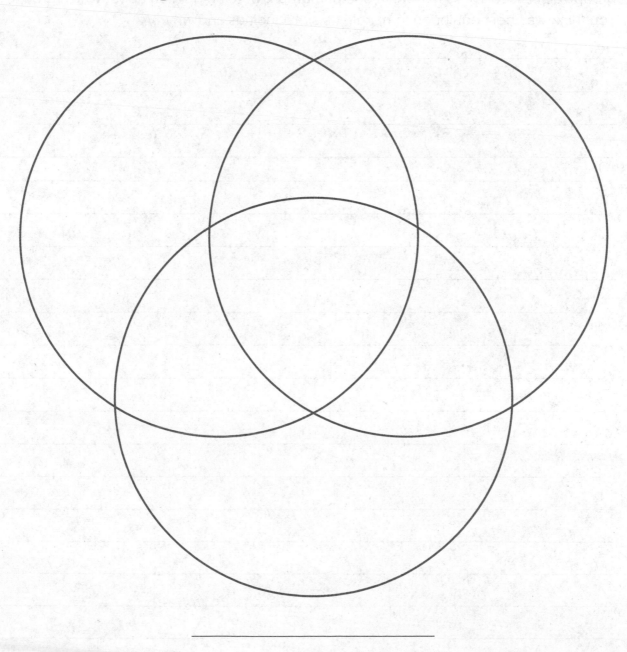

Think About It

Based on your research, what effect did plentiful resources have on the culture of native peoples of the Pacific Coast?

Write About It

Take a Stand

Write and Cite Evidence Compare the artifacts and housing of two Native American groups discussed in this lesson. In one paragraph, write an opinion about which group you think was best equipped to handle its surroundings and why.

_____

_____

_____

_____

_____

_____

_____

_____

_____

_____

_____

_____

_____

_____

_____

_____

_____

_____

Talk About It

Defend Your Claim

In small groups, compare and contrast the Native Americans you learned about this week with the groups from the Southwest deserts in Lesson 2. How does life in a desert and life on the Pacific Coast affect culture?

Geography

Connect to the

Pull It Together

Think about what you have learned about the native peoples of the Pacific Coast. Consider the locations of major cities throughout the world. Explain why people tend to gather in certain areas using what you know about how native peoples of the Pacific Coast were affected by their surroundings.

_____

_____

_____

_____

_____

 Inquiry Project Notes

_____

_____

_____

_____

_____

_____

_____

How Did the Great Plains Influence the Traditions of the People Living There?

Lesson Outcomes

What Am I Learning?

In this lesson, you're going to use your investigative skills to explore the traditions of the native peoples of the Great Plains.

Why Am I Learning It?

Reading and talking about where and how the peoples of the Great Plains lived will help you understand their traditions and ways of life.

How Will I Know That I Learned It?

You will be able to compare and contrast the roles of men and women in Great Plains groups to explain their traditions and ways of life.

Talk About It

COLLABORATE

Look at the Details What does the painting show? What role do you think the buffalo played in the lives of the Great Plains peoples?

The peoples of the Plains depended on buffalo, more accurately called bison. Once horses came to the Americas, Plains hunters could move as fast as the buffalo could run.

Lakota Winter Count

1 Inspect

Look Examine the artifact on the next page. What can it tell you about the traditions of the Lakota people?

Discuss Talk about clues that answer these questions:

- Who made the artifact?
- What is the artifact made of?
- How was the artifact used?

My Notes

_____

_____

_____

_____

_____

_____

_____

_____

_____

_____

_____

The winter count shown on the next page is an illustrated calendar created by the Lakota people of the Great Plains. Each year, Lakota leaders met to discuss the memorable events of the year. A pictograph, or symbol, that describes the most memorable event was then painted on an animal hide. Leaders would name the year based on that event. In this way, the Lakota could reference events by the name of a year. A keeper, who served as the group's historian, kept the winter count safe, year after year. Keepers were usually men.

The artifact is called a "winter count" because the Lakota measured years from the first snowfall of one winter to the first snowfall of the next. This winter count recalls events that occurred between 1800 and 1871. The pictographs appear chronologically, starting at the center of the spiral. Some of the images depict events related to food and hunting, while others show battles with or visits from Europeans. For example:

- The first image on this page shows that Europeans brought striped blankets to the Lakota people in 1853–1854.
- The second image, at the bottom left, shows that the Lakota had plenty of buffalo meat in 1845–1846.
- The third image shows that 30 Lakota were killed by Crow people in 1800–1801.

Winter Count by Lone Dog, 1801–1876

2 Find Evidence

Take Another Look How is the winter count organized? How does this organization help you understand the calendar?

3 Make Connections

Draw Work with a partner. Create your own way of showing important events that have happened at your school over the past two or three weeks. Why did you include the events you did?

Explore Compare and Contrast

You can better understand the ideas in a text if you **compare and contrast** the details the author provides.

1. Read the text.

This will help you understand what the text is about.

2. Think about what the author wants you to know.

When you compare two things, you tell how they are the same. When you contrast things, you tell how they are different. Consider what the author wants you to know about similarities and differences between the roles of men, women, and children in Plains culture.

3. Reread and look for text features.

Authors often use text features when they want to call attention to the similarities and differences between ideas. Analyze text features, looking at headings, bulleted texts, and images.

4. Make notes in a chart.

You can use these notes later to help you remember what you read.

 Based on the text you have read so far, work with your class to fill in some information in the chart below.

Roles for Plains Men	Roles for Plains Women
Men serve as keepers of winter count.	

U.S. History
Making A New Nation
RESEARCH COMPANION

Investigate!

Read pages 36–43 in your Research Companion. Use your investigative skills to look for text evidence that tells you about traditional roles for Great Plains men and women. This chart will help you organize your notes.

Roles for Plains Men	Roles for Plains Women

Think About It

Review your research, and imagine that you are a blogger researching the Plains peoples. What were the most memorable things you learned about the Plains peoples?

Write About It

Compare and Contrast

Write an informative blog post about the various activities and responsibilities of men and women in Native American groups of the Plains.

_____

_____

_____

_____

_____

_____

_____

_____

_____

_____

_____

_____

_____

_____

Talk About It

Explain Your Thinking

Talk to a classmate about your findings. Take turns discussing how the activity helped you understand the differences between the roles of men and women among Plains peoples.

Geography

Connect to the

Pull It Together

Think about the peoples you studied in this lesson. How were their lives shaped by geography?

_____

_____

_____

_____

_____

_____

_____

Inquiry Project Notes

_____

_____

_____

_____

_____

_____

_____

How Did the Eastern Woodlands Impact the Lives of Early People?

Lesson Outcomes

What Am I Learning?

In this lesson, you're going to use your investigative skills to explore how the Native Americans of the Eastern Woodlands survived and lived.

Why Am I Learning It?

Reading and talking about the lives of Native Americans living in this area will help you understand the problem-solving skills that allowed them to survive and thrive.

How Will I Know That I Learned It?

You will be able to describe the problem-solving skills of the Native Americans living in the Eastern Woodlands, state an opinion about the most significant example of problem solving in the region, and support your opinion with evidence.

Talk About It

COLLABORATE

Look at the Details Examine the image and read the caption. Based on the image, what do you think the advantages of the longhouse were? Support your answer with details.

The Iroquois lived in large homes called longhouses that held several families.

1 Inspect

Look Examine the illustration showing the outside and inside of an Iroquois longhouse.

- **Describe** the shape of the longhouse.
- **Identify** the material used to make the longhouse.
- **Discuss** with a partner why the Iroquois would have chosen to live in longhouses.

My Notes

_____

_____

_____

_____

_____

_____

_____

_____

_____

_____

_____

_____

The Iroquois Longhouse

While men sometimes built small wigwams while they were away hunting, the main type of housing for the Iroquois was the longhouse. These large houses took time to build. However, they were built from strong materials so that the Iroquois could live in permanent villages near the land they farmed. The longhouse frame was often made with saplings, which are strong and flexible trees that could curve to make the roof. Large pieces of bark were used for the shingles that covered the walls and roof.

The average Iroquois longhouse was 16 feet wide, 15 feet tall, and 60 feet long, but some houses could be as long as 300 feet. The longhouses had different compartments for different families. When a man married, he moved into his wife's longhouse to live with her extended family. These families were known as clans. As a clan grew, it could add compartments to its longhouse.

2 Find Evidence

Look Notice how the inside of the longhouse is organized. How would this organization make life easier for the people living there?

Examine Notice the bedding and the hallway of the longhouse. How do you think the structure of the longhouse affected the people living there?

3 Make Connections

Talk Discuss with a partner the different parts of the longhouse. What problems does each of these parts solve? Support your opinion with details from the illustration.

Write Describe what you like best about the design of the longhouse.

Explore Problem and Solution

Identifying **problems and solutions** in what you read will help you understand the people you are studying and evaluate their ability to overcome challenges.

1. **Read the text all the way through.**

   This will help you understand what the text is about.

2. **Look at the illustrations and diagrams as well as section titles.**

   This will help you locate and understand important concepts.

3. **Think of the problems faced by the people you are reading about.**

   This will help you recognize solutions when you see them.

4. **Find key facts about the problems and the solutions.**

   While reading, ask yourself, *What details make this problem difficult to solve? What details about the solution make it work well?*

 Based on the text you just read as well as illustrations and diagrams, work with your class to complete the chart below.

Problem	Solution	Key Details
How best to provide shelter		

Investigate!

Read pages 44–53 in your Research Companion. Use your investigative skills to identify problems Native Americans in the Eastern Woodlands faced and the solutions they devised. Use the chart to organize your information.

Problem	Solution	Key Details

Think About It

Based on your research, how well did the Native Americans of the Eastern Woodlands solve their problems?

Write About It

Take a Stand

Write and Cite Evidence In your opinion, what was the most significant example of problem solving in the Eastern Woodlands? List three reasons that support your opinion. Include page references.

_____

_____

_____

_____

_____

_____

_____

_____

_____

_____

_____

_____

_____

_____

_____

_____

Talk About It

Defend Your Claim

Talk with a classmate who chose a different example of problem solving. Take turns discussing your opinions and supporting evidence. Do you agree or disagree with your partner's opinion?

Geography

Connect to the

Pull It Together

Think about the people and events that you have read and talked about in this lesson. How did people solve problems posed by their environment?

_____

_____

_____

_____

_____

 Inquiry Project Notes

_____

_____

_____

_____

_____

_____

_____

Take Action

ESSENTIAL EQ QUESTION

How Were the Lives of Native Peoples Influenced by Where They Lived?

Inquiry Project

Show What Life Was Like . . .

For this project, you will design a museum display for a Native American group from this chapter. Create a poster or diorama showcasing an aspect of their daily lives and demonstrating how location affected the way the group lived. Prepare a museum plaque to describe your visual.

Complete Your Project

Use the checklist below to evaluate your project. If you left anything out, now's your chance to fix it!

- ☐ Tell which Native American group you have researched.

- ☐ In your poster or diorama, show a specific aspect of the group's daily or spiritual life or an aspect of its culture.

- ☐ Include details that show a deep understanding of your research topic.

- ☐ Support the information about your topic with strong evidence.

- ☐ Make sure to clearly communicate information on your poster or diorama.

Share Your Project

Talk about your project with a partner. Take turns explaining what you learned from your research. Then choose two important details to share with the rest of the class.

Reflect on Your Project

Think about the work you did in this chapter and on your project. Use the questions below to help guide your thoughts.

1. Why did you choose the Native American group that you researched?

_____

2. How did you conduct your research? Is there anything you'd do

differently next time? _____

_____

3. How did you make sure that your sources were reliable? _____

_____

Chapter Connections

Use pictures, words, or both to reflect on what you learned in this chapter.

The most interesting thing I learned:

Something I learned from a classmate:

A connection I can make with my own life:

How Does Where We Live IMPACT US?

Regional Differences

You've read about how the lives of different Native American groups were shaped by the regions in which they lived. Climate, vegetation, and geography had an impact on their clothing, housing, diets, and traditions. Now you'll read about regions in the Western Hemisphere and investigate how geography, climate, and vegetation impact our lives. You'll also think about how people impact the regions in which they live.

Talk About It

The Same and Different

The photos show two types of desert dwellings. One is an ancient pueblo. The other is a modern version of a pueblo. What similarities and differences do you see? How do you think the ancient pueblo design is still useful in the desert region today?

Ancient pueblo dwelling in Mesa Verde National Park

A modern home built in the pueblo style

Investigate!

Read about the physical, climate, and vegetation regions of the Western Hemisphere on pages 56–65 in your Research Companion. As you read, think about the question:

How Does Where We Live Impact Us?

Think About It

You've read and talked about different physical, climate, and vegetation regions in the Western Hemisphere. Now think about life where you are. How do the land, climate, and vegetation impact people's lives where you live?

Write About It

Write and Cite Evidence

Write a short description or draw a picture of the land, climate, and vegetation in your area. Then describe how these things affect the lives of the people where you live. Consider things such as the clothes people wear at different times of the year, what activities people do outdoors, how people get around the area, and the work people do.

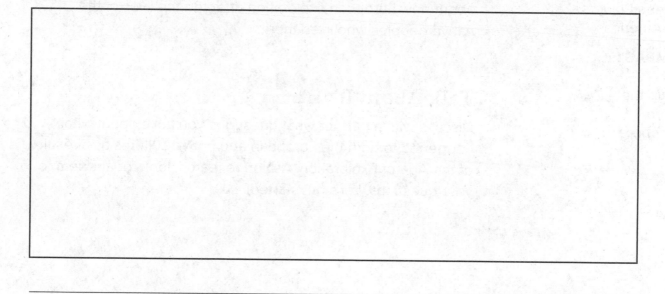

Talk About It

Defend Your Claim

Talk to a classmate and compare your ideas about how land, climate, and vegetation affect your daily life. What similarities and differences did you each find?

The Age of Exploration

What Happened When Diverse Cultures Crossed Paths?

In this chapter, you'll read about why European powers decided to explore and claim parts of the Americas. You will also read about how European exploration affected the lives of the native peoples who lived there.

Talk About It

Discuss with a partner what questions you have about what happened to both the European and native cultures as a result of the Age of Exploration. As you research, look for answers to your questions. Let's get started!

Inquiry Project

European Explorers: Collect Them All!

Choose a European explorer discussed in this chapter, other than Christopher Columbus. Create a "trading card" for this explorer that includes an image depicting the explorer on the front. On the back, include important "statistics" or facts, such as where and when he was born, what led him to explore the Americas, and how his expedition impacted his country and the native peoples he interacted with. Then write a conclusion evaluating whether his actions were mostly positive or mostly negative.

Project Checklist

☐ **Analyze** the task. Make sure you understand what you are expected to do.

☐ **Choose** an explorer from the chapter.

☐ **Conduct** research into the explorer's background and expedition. Take notes.

☐ **Create** an explorer trading card.

☐ **Write** a conclusion that explains whether his actions were mostly positive or mostly negative.

My Research Plan

Write down any research questions you have that will help you plan your project. You can add questions as you carry out your research.

_____

_____

_____

_____

_____

Explore Words

Complete this chapter's Word Rater. Write notes as you learn more about each word.

charter

My Notes

☐ Know It!

☐ Heard It!

☐ Don't Know It!

_____

_____

_____

claim

My Notes

☐ Know It!

☐ Heard It!

☐ Don't Know It!

_____

_____

_____

colony

My Notes

☐ Know It!

☐ Heard It!

☐ Don't Know It!

_____

_____

_____

conquest

My Notes

☐ Know It!

☐ Heard It!

☐ Don't Know It!

_____

_____

_____

diverse

My Notes

☐ Know It!

☐ Heard It!

☐ Don't Know It!

_____

_____

_____

merchants

My Notes

☐ Know It!

☐ Heard It!

☐ Don't Know It!

_____

_____

_____

navigation

My Notes

☐ Know It!

☐ Heard It!

☐ Don't Know It!

_____

_____

_____

resistance

My Notes

☐ Know It!

☐ Heard It!

☐ Don't Know It!

_____

_____

_____

settlement

My Notes

☐ Know It!

☐ Heard It!

☐ Don't Know It!

_____

_____

_____

warship

My Notes

☐ Know It!

☐ Heard It!

☐ Don't Know It!

_____

_____

_____

Lesson Outcomes

What Am I Learning?

In this lesson, you're going to use your investigative skills to learn how and why Spanish explorers first came to the Americas.

Why Am I Learning It?

Reading and talking about the lesson will help you understand the actions of early Spanish explorers, such as Christopher Columbus, and how they affected the development of colonial America.

How Will I Know That I Learned It?

You will be able to use cause and effect to understand the developments that encouraged early Spanish explorers, such as Columbus, to sail to the Americas. You will be able to write an advertisement describing one of these technological developments and explaining how it would help an explorer on his voyage.

Talk About It

COLLABORATE

Examine the Details Read the English translation of Columbus's letter. What does it tell you about the first Spanish explorers who came to the Americas?

In Their Words... Christopher Columbus

. . . I gave [the inhabitants] many beautiful and pleasing things, which I had brought with me, for no return whatever, in order to win their affection, and that they might become Christians and inclined to love our King and Queen and Princes and all the people of Spain; and that they might be eager to search for and gather and give to us what they abound in and we greatly need.

—from a letter Columbus wrote to Queen Isabella and King Ferdinand as soon as he returned from his first voyage in 1493

1 Inspect

Look Examine this image. What does it depict?

- **Underline** words you don't know that are used as labels.
- **Circle** parts of the image that show you what those labels indicate.
- **Discuss** with a partner the kind of ship that Columbus sailed to the Americas.

My Notes

_____

_____

_____

_____

_____

_____

_____

_____

_____

_____

_____

_____

_____

Diagram of a Caravel

The caravel was a small, light sailing ship. It was designed by the Portuguese and used by the Spanish in the late 1400s. Its lateen (triangular) and square sails caught the wind to help the ship travel faster. The caravel had a stern, or rear, rudder that helped it steer easily. It had a shallow keel, or bottom, that allowed it to go closer to shore than most other ships. It also had a large cargo hold to store supplies that were needed for a long journey. The *Niña* and the *Pinta*, two of the ships Columbus used to sail to the Americas, were caravels.

Lateen Sails

Stern

Rudder

Keel

Copyright © McGraw-Hill Education

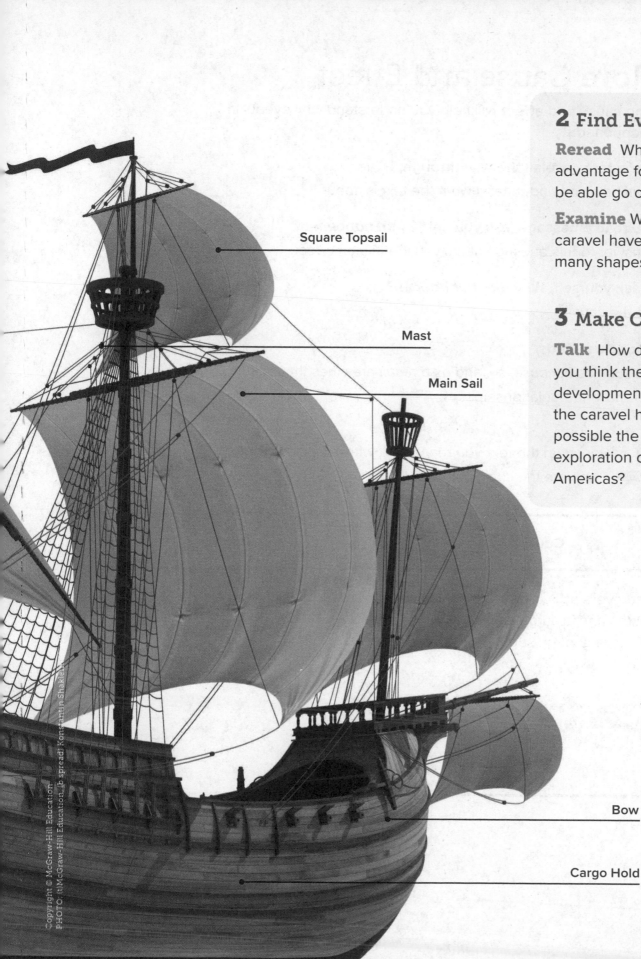

Square Topsail

Mast

Main Sail

Bow

Cargo Hold

2 Find Evidence

Reread Why would it be an advantage for the caravel to be able go closer to shore?

Examine Why might the caravel have had sails of so many shapes and sizes?

3 Make Connections

Talk How do you think the development of the caravel helped make possible the Spanish exploration of the Americas?

COLLABORATE

Explore Cause and Effect

Identifying **cause and effect** will help you understand why events in history happened.

1. **Read the text once all the way through.**

   This will help you understand what the text is about.

2. **As you read a passage, ask yourself, *What happened?***

   The answer to this question helps you identify an effect.

3. **Then ask yourself, *Why did that happen?***

   This is the cause.

4. **Look for clue words.**

   Words such as *because, so,* and *as a result* are clues that point to a cause-and-effect relationship.

Based on the text you read, work with your class to complete the chart below.

Cause	Effect
The caravel's sails allowed the ship to go faster, and its large cargo hold could store enough supplies for long journeys.	

Investigate!

Read pages 72–81 in your Research Companion. Use your investigative skills to identify the developments that led to Spanish exploration of the Americas. Use the chart below to organize the information.

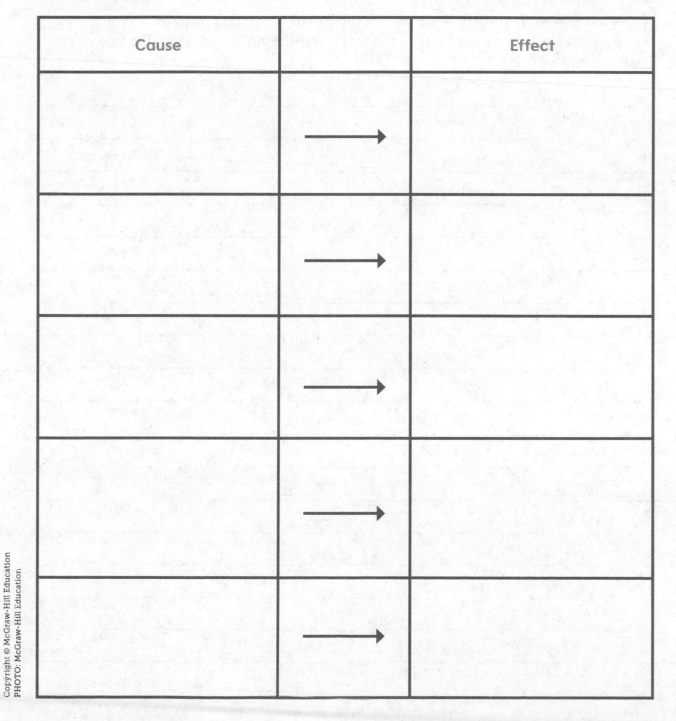

Cause		Effect
	→	
	→	
	→	
	→	
	→	

Think About It

Review your research about the developments that encouraged Spanish exploration of the Americas. Which invention do you think was the most important? Why?

Write About It

Be Persuasive

Write an Advertisement Write an advertisement describing how the invention you chose works and why an explorer would find it useful. Find an image on the Internet to illustrate your ad.

_____

_____

_____

_____

_____

_____

_____

_____

_____

_____

_____

_____

_____

_____

_____

_____

Talk About It

Defend Your Choice

Review the goals of Spanish explorers. Then discuss how the invention you chose would help them achieve these goals.

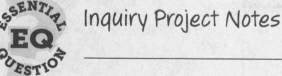 **Connect to the**

Pull It Together

Explain how the invention you chose helped Spanish explorers like Christopher Columbus and how it might have affected the exploration and development of colonial America.

_____

_____

_____

_____

_____

_____

_____

_____

Inquiry Project Notes

_____

_____

_____

How Did Spanish Exploration Change the Lives of People in the Americas?

Lesson Outcomes

What Am I Learning?

In this lesson, you're going to use your investigative skills to learn how Spanish contact and exploration in the Americas changed the lives of the native peoples living there.

Why Am I Learning It?

Reading and talking about the effects of Spanish contact and exploration will help you understand changes that took place and that helped shape the Americas in the future.

How Will I Know That I Learned It?

You will be able to identify the causes and explain the effects of the Columbian Exchange and of Spanish conquest, exploration, and colonization of the Americas.

Talk About It

COLLABORATE

Look at the Details Examine the image of Cortés and his men. Based on this painting, do you predict their interactions with native peoples will end peacefully or violently?

Hernan Cortés at Vera Cruz in 1519, where he decided to found a village.

1 Inspect

Look Examine this map. What types of items does it show?

- **Underline** plants that traveled between the Americas and Europe.
- **Circle** animals that traveled between the Americas and Europe.
- **Discuss** with a partner the effects that these items might have had on the peoples involved in the exchange.

My Notes

_____

_____

_____

_____

_____

_____

_____

_____

_____

_____

_____

_____

_____

The Columbian Exchange

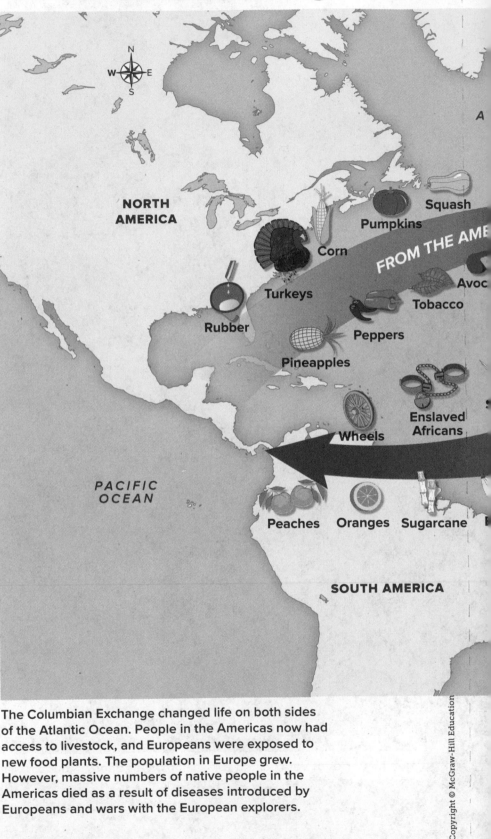

The Columbian Exchange changed life on both sides of the Atlantic Ocean. People in the Americas now had access to livestock, and Europeans were exposed to new food plants. The population in Europe grew. However, massive numbers of native people in the Americas died as a result of diseases introduced by Europeans and wars with the European explorers.

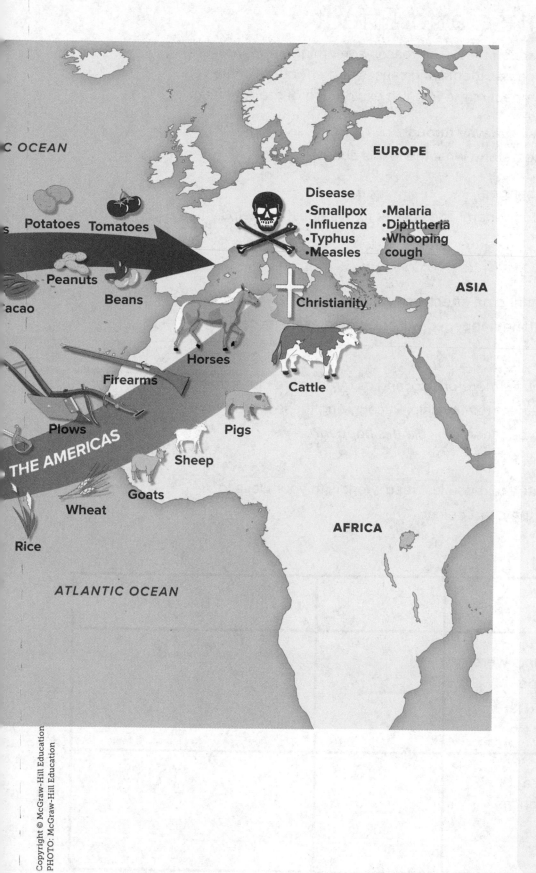

OCEAN

EUROPE

Potatoes Tomatoes

Peanuts

Cacao   Beans

Disease
•Smallpox   •Malaria
•Influenza •Diphtheria
•Typhus   •Whooping
•Measles   cough

ASIA

Christianity

Horses

Firearms

Cattle

Plows

Pigs

THE AMERICAS

Sheep

Goats

Wheat

AFRICA

Rice

ATLANTIC OCEAN

2 Find Evidence

Look Again Beyond items such as food and technology, what other things were exchanged? Were all of them beneficial?

3 Make Connections

Talk Which items do you think had the biggest effect on the lives of natives of the Americas? Why?

COLLABORATE

Explore Cause and Effect

A **cause** is an event or action that is the reason something happens. An **effect** is the result of a cause. Identifying causes and effects will help you better understand the impact of the Spanish exploration of the Americas.

1. Read the text once all the way through.

This will help you understand what the text is about.

2. Watch for specific changes.

Ask yourself, *What happened?* The answer to this question helps you identify an effect.

3. Look for explanations.

When you have identified an effect, ask yourself, *Why did this happen?* Knowing why something happened will help you explain its cause.

4. Look for clue words.

Words such as *because, therefore, so,* and *as a result* are clues that signal a cause-and-effect relationship. Recognizing these words will help you answer the question *Why did this happen?*

COLLABORATE
Based on the text you just read, work with your class to complete the chart below.

Causes		Effects
Many new food plants were introduced to Europe.	→	
Many diseases were brought to the Americas.	→	

Investigate!

Read pages 82–93 in your Research Companion. Use your investigative skills to determine causes and effects of Spanish conquest and colonization. Use the diagram below to organize the information.

Causes		Effects
	→	
	→	
	→	
	→	
	→	
	→	

Think About It

Your teacher will assign one of these explorers or conquistadors that you read about: Juan Ponce de Léon, Hernan Cortés, Francisco Pizarro, Alvar Nuñez Cabeza de Vaca, Hernando de Soto, or Francisco Vásquez de Coronado. Based on what you have read, what effect did this person have on Spain's colonization of the Americas?

Write About It

Write an Essay

Choose a *different* explorer or conquistador than the one you were assigned. Write a three-paragraph informational essay about the impact the explorer or conquistador had on the native peoples of the Americas.

_____

_____

_____

_____

_____

_____

_____

_____

_____

_____

_____

_____

_____

_____

Talk About It

Share Your Ideas

Form a group with other students who wrote about the same Spanish explorer or conquistador. Discuss what was most significant about his actions.

Connect to the **EQ**

History

Consider a Different Outcome

Think about the details in the material you have read. From those details, how do you imagine native peoples' lives would have been different had the Spanish not arrived in the Americas? Would they have been better off?

_____

_____

_____

_____

_____

Inquiry Project Notes

_____

_____

_____

_____

_____

_____

_____

How Did European Exploration Affect the Americas?

Lesson Outcomes

What Am I Learning?

In this lesson, you're going to use your investigative skills to explore how European exploration and settlement affected the Americas.

Why Am I Learning It?

Reading and talking about European exploration and settlement in the Americas will help you understand how the colonial period began and how native peoples were impacted.

How Will I Know That I Learned It?

You will be able to show an understanding of how Europeans affected the Americas by examining maps, and you will be able to demonstrate an understanding of how Europeans interacted with native peoples by writing about those encounters.

Talk About It

COLLABORATE

Look at the Details What seems to be happening in the picture? How do the people seem to feel about each other?

Jacques Cartier meets Native Americans in what is now Montreal, Canada.

1 Inspect

Look Observe the map. What part of the world does it show?

Read Examine the map title, key, and text. What is the map about? What do the colored lines represent?

Circle Mark key information on the map and in the text.

- important words and dates
- names of explorers
- major labels on the map

Discuss What do you think the Northwest Passage was? Did explorers succeed in finding it?

My Notes

_____

_____

_____

_____

_____

_____

_____

_____

_____

_____

A Shortcut to Asia

Many of the European explorers who reached North America between the late 1400s and early 1600s were really trying to get to Asia. Trade with Asia could be very profitable, especially when spices were involved. However, getting to Asia by sailing around Africa was difficult and dangerous. European rulers wanted to see if there was another way there.

The voyages shown on the map on the next page were paid for by the governments of England, France, and the Netherlands. The voyages took place between the years 1497 and 1611.

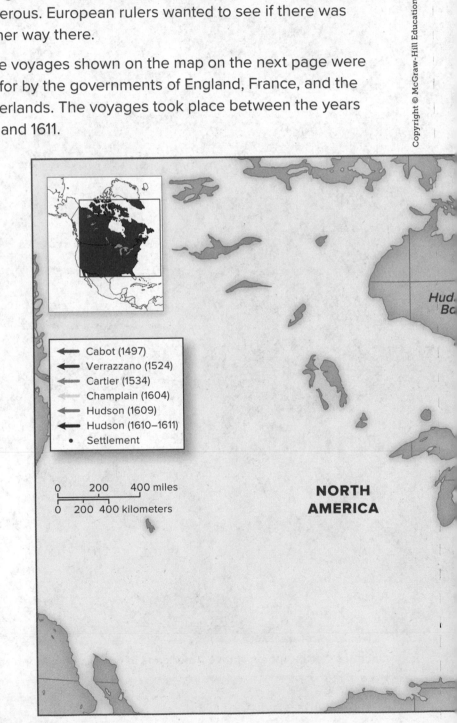

- ← Cabot (1497)
- ← Verrazzano (1524)
- ← Cartier (1534)
- ← Champlain (1604)
- ← Hudson (1609)
- ← Hudson (1610–1611)
- • Settlement

```
0      200      400 miles
0   200  400 kilometers
```

NORTH AMERICA

Hud
Ba

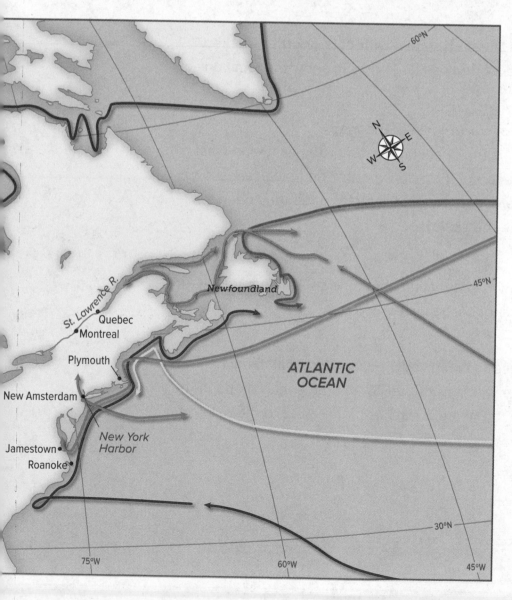

Europeans Search for a Northwest Passage, 1497–1611

St. Lawrence R.
Quebec
Montreal
Plymouth
New Amsterdam
Jamestown
Roanoke
New York Harbor
Newfoundland

ATLANTIC OCEAN

60°N
45°N
30°N
75°W
60°W
45°W

2 Find Evidence

Look Closely Using the information from the map, which explorer spent the longest time searching for the Northwest Passage?

Analyze Compare the route of Cartier in 1534 and the route of Hudson in 1610 with the other four routes. What makes those two routes different?

3 Make Connections

Discuss Talk with a partner. Give your opinion of which explorer came closest to finding a Northwest Passage. Give reasons to support your opinion.

Reading Maps

Maps can provide many types of information. Look at the map on the following page, and think about what information is being provided.

To analyze a map, follow these steps:

1. **Read the title of the map.**
    This should give you a good idea of the most important information the mapmaker is trying to provide.

2. **Read the labels on the map.**
    Note any differences in the size or style of the type. Larger labels may show major regions. Italic type may show bodies of water or other land features.

3. **Look for any places on the map shown with dots or other markers.**
    For example, mapmakers often use large dots to show the locations of major cities.

4. **Identify the compass rose and scale of the map.**
    The compass rose shows the directions north, south, east, and west. On almost all maps, the top of the map is north. The map scale shows the lengths used to represent miles or kilometers. You may need to use a ruler to determine the scale.

5. **Look for a map key.**
    This is a box that provides information about the special features of a map, such as color coding, dashed lines, or icons.

COLLABORATE

As a class, use the map key on page 72 to match each colored route with its explorer. Then on the map on pages 72–73, write the name of each explorer close to the colored line that shows his route.

Investigate!

Read pages 94–103 in your Research Companion. Use your investigative skills to look for text evidence that helps you fill in the missing information in the map key. Write the name of the country that claimed the territory shown by each color on the map.

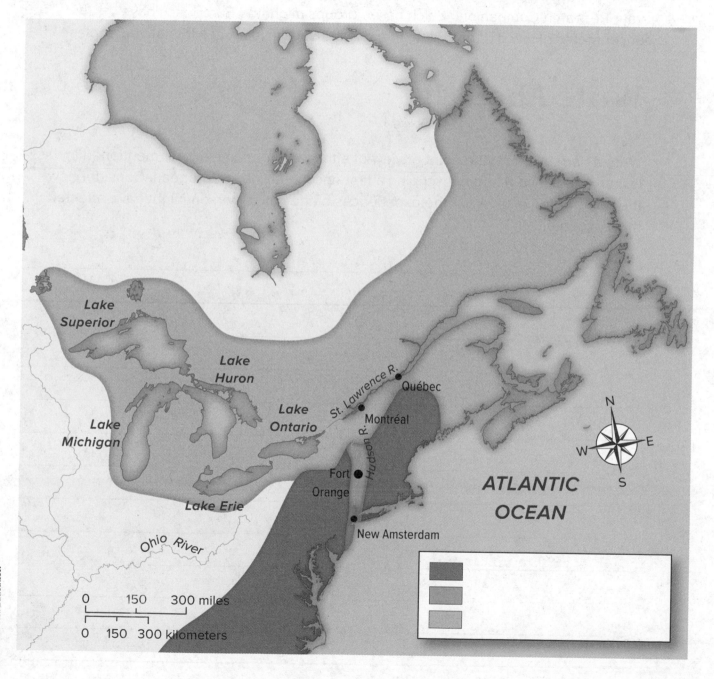

Lake Superior

Lake Huron

Lake Michigan

Lake Ontario

Lake Erie

St. Lawrence R.

Québec

Montréal

Hudson R.

Fort Orange

New Amsterdam

Ohio River

ATLANTIC OCEAN

N E S W

0   150   300 miles

0   150   300 kilometers

Think About It

Review your research. Based on what you have read, what were the exploration goals in the Americas of the Netherlands, France, and England?

Talk About It

COLLABORATE

Compare the maps of European settlements in this lesson with the map on page 45 in your Research Companion. Which native groups might the Europeans have encountered? How did the Dutch, French, and English interact with native peoples?

Write About It

Narrative

Write a narrative from the point of view of either a European explorer mentioned in this lesson or a native person describing a first encounter with a European. Consider how the goals of the explorer or the experiences of the native person might have affected this encounter.

_____

_____

_____

_____

_____

_____

_____

_____

_____

_____

_____

History # Connect to the **EQ** *ESSENTIAL QUESTION*

Contrast

Looking back over the chapter, discuss how the relationships between Native Americans and the various European explorers differed.

_____

_____

_____

_____

_____

_____

_____

_____

_____

_____

_____

Inquiry Project Notes

_____

_____

_____

_____

_____

_____

_____

What Happened When Diverse Cultures Crossed Paths?

Inquiry Project

Tell How Diverse Cultures Connected . . .

For this project, you will create a trading card for a European explorer other than Columbus. Finish by writing a conclusion evaluating whether his actions were mostly positive or mostly negative.

Complete Your Project

Use the checklist below to evaluate your project. If you left anything out, now's your chance to fix it!

☐ On the front of your card, show an image of the explorer you researched.

☐ On the back of your card, show key facts about your explorer such as where and when he was born, what led him to explore the Americas, and how his expedition impacted his country and also native peoples.

☐ Include a summary of how your explorer's actions were mostly positive or mostly negative.

☐ Support the information about your explorer with strong evidence.

☐ Clearly communicate information on your card.

Share Your Project

Project or hand out copies of the front and back of your trading card to classmates. Talk about the most important facts about your explorer. Provide details in logical order, such as time order or cause and effect. Refer to your trading card often, using it to illustrate the details in your presentation.

Reflect on Your Project

Think about the work you did in this chapter and on your project. Use the questions below to help guide your thoughts.

1. Why did you choose the explorer that you researched?

_____

2. Would you conduct your research differently next time? How?

_____

_____

3. How did you make sure that your sources were reliable?

_____

_____

Chapter Connections

Use pictures, words, or both to reflect on what you learned in this chapter.

The most interesting thing I learned:

Something I learned from a classmate:

A connection I can make with my own life:

Why Do Products and Ideas Move From Place to Place?

Markets and Resources

When Europeans arrived in the Western Hemisphere in the late 1400s, they were looking to trade. Trade with Asia had brought vast riches to Europe, and Europeans were trying to find a shorter route to India and other Asian countries. The European countries that sent explorers westward included Spain, England, France, the Netherlands, Portugal, and Sweden.

Now you'll investigate the impact of foreign trade today.

Talk About It COLLABORATE

Discuss

Look at the ships. The two photos show a ship from the time of European exploration of the Americas and a ship from today. Both of these ships carry goods for trade. What products do you think we get from ships from foreign countries today? Why do you think we need to import these products?

Investigate!

Read about foreign trade on pages 106–109 in your Research Companion. As you read, think about the question, **Why Do Products and Ideas Move From Place to Place?**

Think About It

Think about a popular product or service that people in the United States import. Why do we import this product? Then think about a product or service that the United States exports. Why do other countries want this product?

Write About It

Write and Cite Evidence

Is trade good for our economy and our lives? Describe any benefits and drawbacks of trade. Then list three reasons that support your opinion. Include evidence in your reasons.

_____

_____

_____

_____

Reasons

1. _____

_____

2. _____

_____

3. _____

_____

Talk About It COLLABORATE

Defend Your Claim

Talk to a classmate about your opinion on trade. Take turns discussing your opinion and supporting evidence. Do you agree or disagree with your partner's opinion? Why?

A Changing Continent

ESSENTIAL EQ QUESTION

What Is the Impact of People Settling in a New Place?

In this chapter, you'll learn how European settlements affected the land and native peoples of North America. You'll learn about how England, France, and Spain competed for land and power in North America, and you'll identify how relations with Native American groups influenced the success of each settlement.

Talk About It COLLABORATE

Discuss with a partner what questions you have about how European settlements developed in North America and how those settlements affected the continent as well as Native Americans. As you research, look for answers to your questions. Let's get started!

Inquiry Project

Tell Both Sides of the Story

Write a short narrative that illustrates the relations between a specific group of European settlers and the Native Americans they encountered. Describe events clearly from both sides, using effective dialogue and descriptions. Identify the effects of those relations on the Native Americans' way of life as well as the benefits or setbacks the Europeans experienced.

Project Checklist

☐ **Analyze** the task. Make sure you understand what you are expected to do.

☐ **Choose** a settlement discussed in the chapter.

☐ **Conduct** research into the settlement's origin and relations with local Native Americans. Take notes.

☐ **Write** a narrative about these relations, using details and facts from the text.

☐ **Work** with a small group to read aloud each other's narratives.

☐ **Discuss** the effects of the settlement's relations with the Native Americans.

My Research Plan

Write down any research questions you have that will help you plan your project. You can add questions as you carry out your research.

_____

_____

_____

_____

Explore Words

Complete this chapter's Word Rater. Write notes
as you learn more about each word.

assembly

My Notes

☐ Know It!
☐ Heard It!
☐ Don't Know It!

_____
_____
_____

cash crop

My Notes

☐ Know It!
☐ Heard It!
☐ Don't Know It!

_____
_____
_____

commerce

My Notes

☐ Know It!
☐ Heard It!
☐ Don't Know It!

_____
_____
_____

covenant

My Notes

☐ Know It!
☐ Heard It!
☐ Don't Know It!

_____
_____
_____

demand

My Notes

☐ Know It!
☐ Heard It!
☐ Don't Know It!

_____
_____
_____

dissension

My Notes

☐ Know It!

_____

☐ Heard It!

_____

☐ Don't Know It!

_____

encomiendas

My Notes

☐ Know It!

_____

☐ Heard It!

_____

☐ Don't Know It!

_____

environment

My Notes

☐ Know It!

_____

☐ Heard It!

_____

☐ Don't Know It!

_____

missionary

My Notes

☐ Know It!

_____

☐ Heard It!

_____

☐ Don't Know It!

_____

proprietor

My Notes

☐ Know It!

_____

☐ Heard It!

_____

☐ Don't Know It!

_____

How Did Early English Settlers Cooperate and Clash with Native Americans?

Lesson Outcomes

What Am I Learning?

In this lesson, you're going to use your investigative skills to understand the history of England's first permanent colony in North America and how the colonists affected and were affected by Native Americans.

Why Am I Learning It?

Reading and talking about the Jamestown colony will help you learn how different cultures interact and how actions and decisions are connected.

How Will I Know That I Learned It?

You will be able to explain the causes and effects of Jamestown's failures and successes.

Talk About It

COLLABORATE

Look at the Map What features do you notice about the settlement? What is the importance of these features?

James Fort at Jamestown settlement

The Starving Time

1 Inspect

Read First read the introductory text, and then read the quotation in the Primary Source box. How are they related?

- **Circle** words used in ways that are different from the ways they are most often used. Try to determine their meaning from context.

- **Discuss** with a group whether the Starving Time could have been prevented if John Smith had not been injured.

My Notes

_____

_____

_____

_____

_____

_____

_____

_____

_____

_____

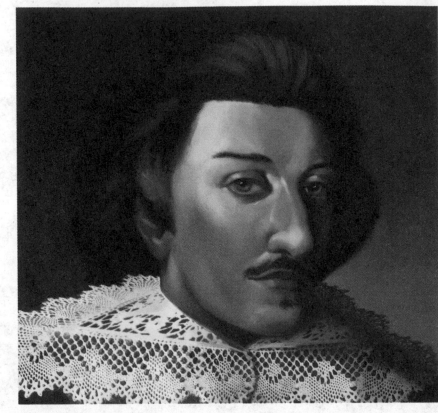

George Percy

In 1609, Captain John Smith was wounded in a gunpowder accident. His injuries forced him to return to England, and a noble named George Percy took his place as the leader of the Jamestown colony. Smith had played a key role in improving relations with the Powhatan people and ensuring the colonists worked hard. Without him, they were unprepared for a drought later that year, and Chief Powhatan refused to help them. Although Chief Powhatan had liked and respected Smith, he did not feel the same about other settlers. Chief Powhatan was concerned that the settlers wanted to take over his people's land, thereby displacing the Powhatan people. Seeing the colony as weak and vulnerable, the Powhatan leader decided to starve the settlers into abandoning their colony, ordering his men to kill any colonist attempting to hunt or gather food outside of the fort. By the spring of 1610, only 60 colonists remained at Jamestown.

In Their Words... George Percy

Jamestown "Starving Time"

Now all of us at James Town, beginning to feel that sharp prick of hunger which no man truly describe but he which has tasted the bitterness thereof, a world of miseries ensued as the sequel will express unto you, in so much that some to satisfy their hunger have robbed the store for the which I caused them to be executed.

Then having fed upon horses and other beasts as long as they lasted, we were glad to make shift with vermin as dogs, cats, rats, and mice. All was fish that came to net to satisfy cruel hunger as to eat boots, shoes, or any other leather some could come by, and, those being spent and devoured, some were enforced to search the woods and to feed upon serpents and snakes and to dig the earth for wild and unknown roots, where many of our men were cut off of and slain by the savages.

—from George Percy's *A True Relation—A Trewe Relacyon*, written in the mid-1620s.

2 Find Evidence

Reread What details does George Percy include in his account to support the idea that the colony was starving? Why are these details effective?

What is meant by the statement "All was fish that came to net to satisfy cruel hunger"? Is Percy referring to actual fish?

3 Make Connections

Talk What was the main cause of the Starving Time? Discuss and defend your opinion with your group.

COLLABORATE

What long-term effects do you think the Starving Time had on the colony?

Explore Cause and Effect

Some of the events you will read about in this lesson have cause-and-effect relationships. To better understand history, it is important to know about cause and effect. The causes of historical events explain why things happened, and the effects of events show why the events are important to people afterwards.

1. **Look for transitions related to causes and effects.**

   Because, therefore, as a result, in order to, and similar transitional words and phrases can indicate cause-and-effect relationships.

2. **Take note of chronology.**

   Texts will often present cause-and-effect relationships in the order that the two events happen. This is not always true, though, so be careful.

3. **Analyze the events.**

   Would an event have happened without this particular cause? Would the effect have been the same if the earlier event had never happened? Ask yourself questions like these to determine how strong the relationship between two events is.

4. **Note that an event may have more than one cause or effect.**

   COLLABORATE Based on the text you just read, work with your class to complete the chart below.

Cause		Effect
John Smith returned to England.	→	

Investigate!

Read pages 118–127 in your Research Companion. Use your investigative skills to identify cause-and-effect relationships in the text. Find events in the text that led to improved or worsened relations between the colonists and the Powhatan. Each event will be the "cause," while what happened as a result of each event is the "effect." Use this information to fill in the graphic organizer below.

Cause		Effect
	➡	
	➡	
	➡	
	➡	

Think About It

Review your research. Based on the information you have gathered, did the settlers' relationship with Native Americans ultimately help or hurt the Jamestown Colony?

Write About It

Take a Stand

Write and Cite Evidence Defend your idea by identifying at least three examples from Jamestown's history that indicate whether the relationship with Native Americans helped or harmed the Jamestown settlement. Use evidence from the text to support your opinion.

_____

_____

_____

_____

_____

_____

_____

_____

_____

_____

_____

_____

_____

_____

_____

_____

Talk About It

Defend Your Claim

Choose a partner who disagrees with you about the relationship between the Powhatan and the settlers. Work together to outline your difference of opinion. Did your partner's claim change your thinking about your own claim?

History

Connect to the

Pull It Together

Think about the changing relationship between the English settlers and the Powhatan people. How might this relationship have shaped future interaction between English colonists and Native Americans?

_____

_____

_____

_____

_____

_____

_____

Inquiry Project Notes

_____

_____

_____

_____

_____

How Did Early European Settlers Compete with One Another and Native Americans?

Lesson Outcomes

What Am I Learning?

In this lesson, you're going to use your investigative skills to explore how European colonists competed with one another and Native Americans.

Why Am I Learning It?

Reading and talking about competition among European settlers and Native Americans will help you understand how and why the different groups attempted to gain power over one another.

How Will I Know That I Learned It?

You will be able to explain the different strategies of European and Native American groups in the Americas and evaluate the economic results of their efforts.

Talk About It

COLLABORATE

Look at the Details Which groups are involved in the battle? Who is fighting whom?

Samuel de Champlain's men allied with Algonquin people fighting an Iroquois war party

The Saint Lawrence: At the Heart of New France

1 Inspect

Read Look at the title. What do you think this text will be about?

- **Circle** words you don't know.
- **Underline** clues that help answer these questions:
  - Where is the Saint Lawrence River?
  - Who used the river?
  - Why was it important?

My Notes

_____

_____

_____

_____

_____

_____

_____

_____

_____

_____

_____

_____

_____

The Saint Lawrence River connects the Great Lakes to the Atlantic Ocean. French explorers hoped that the Saint Lawrence could take them all the way across North America. The river did not do so. However, it did supply a route for trade and exploration of Canada and what is now the northern United States.

Samuel de Champlain was one of the first Europeans to sail the river, in 1603. At the time, he called it the River of Canada. Champlain published a report of his travels in France. Champlain's writings inspired more support for the exploration of the Saint Lawrence. In 1608, Champlain and a group of colonists settled along the river, naming the region Quebec.

The colony of New France used this lengthy waterway to transport furs and other trade goods. From trading posts as far inland as Chicago and Detroit, the colonists could easily move goods to and across the Atlantic Ocean. Since people tend to live close to water, the Saint Lawrence also allowed the French to establish relationships with many of the Native American groups of the region. This Saint Lawrence trade network played a major role in the economy of New France.

Samuel de Champlain arrives at the site of Quebec City along the Saint Lawrence River.

2 Find Evidence

Reread List three reasons why the Saint Lawrence River was important to New France.

Underline the names of places connected by the Saint Lawrence River.

3 Make Connections

Talk Do you think Native Americans likely benefited or suffered as a result of the Saint Lawrence trade network?

How does the picture help you understand how French sailors navigated the Saint Lawrence?

Explore Main Ideas and Details

The author's point is the **main idea** of a text. This is what the author wants readers to understand. He or she supports the main idea with **details**. Sometimes a text has more than one main idea. Details are facts and evidence about the topic.

To understand main ideas and details:

1. **Read the text all the way through.**
   This will help you understand what the text is about.

2. **Look at section titles.**
   These can be clues to how the text is organized and can help you understand what each section is mostly about.

3. **Reread the first and last paragraphs in each section.**
   These paragraphs often include the main idea or give you clues about what the main idea is.

4. **Identify key details.**
   Look for important information, facts, or evidence that seem to support the main idea.

 Based on the text you just read, work with your class to complete the chart below.

Main Idea	Details
The Saint Lawrence River played a major role in the development of New France.	

Investigate!

Read pages 128–139 in your Research Companion. Use your investigative skills to look for text evidence that tells you about the goals or motivations of the European nations for colonizing North America. This chart will help you organize your notes.

Main Idea	Details

Think About It

Review your research. Based on the information you have gathered, what do you think European powers wanted most from North America? How did that affect the people who already lived in North America?

Write About It

Write a Story

Write a short story from the point of view of a Native American or a colonist. Explain who you are, where you come from, and how your life was affected by European colonization of North America. Use details from the text in your story.

_____

_____

_____

_____

_____

_____

_____

_____

_____

_____

_____

_____

_____

_____

_____

Talk About It

COLLABORATE

Compare Your Accounts

Work with a partner who has chosen to write from a different point of view. What were the costs of European settlement of North America? What were the benefits?

Economics

Connect to the ESSENTIAL EQ QUESTION

Compare

Think about the lasting effects of European settlement of North America. How did trade affect the relationship between Europeans and Native Americans?

_____

_____

_____

_____

_____

_____

_____

_____

_____

 Inquiry Project Notes

ESSENTIAL EQ QUESTION

_____

_____

_____

_____

_____

What Was Life Like for People in New England?

Lesson Outcomes

What Am I Learning?

In this lesson, you're going to use your investigative skills to explore what life was like in New England for settlers and Native Americans.

Why Am I Learning It?

Reading and talking about what life was like in New England will help you learn more about how people interacted in colonial times.

How Will I Know That I Learned It?

You will be able to identify the main idea and key details about the challenges facing colonists and Native Americans in New England and then write an essay about the two biggest challenges facing those peoples.

Talk About It

COLLABORATE

Look at the Map Who are these people? How are they interacting with each other? How do you know?

The First Thanksgiving at Plymouth
by Jennie Augusta Brownscombe

The Bounty of North America

Colonists like William Hilton faced many hardships on their journey to North America. They traveled for two months on cramped ships across a rough and stormy ocean. They endured disease, hunger, and seasickness. With luck, they were able to build a settlement without encountering more dangers. Often, however, the colonists were unable to grow food, or they clashed with Native Americans when they tried to settle on lands on which Native Americans already lived. Luckily, Hilton managed to make a good start at his new life.

PRIMARY SOURCE

Loving Cousin,

At our arrival in New Plymouth, in New England, we found all our friends and planters in good health, though they were left sick and weak, with very small means; the Indians round about us peaceable and friendly; the country very pleasant and temperate, yielding naturally, of itself, great store of fruits, as vines of divers sorts in great abundance.

There is likewise walnuts, chestnuts, small nuts and plums, with much variety of flowers, roots and herbs, no less pleasant than wholesome and profitable. No place hath more gooseberries and strawberries, nor better. Timber of all sorts you have in England doth cover the land, that affords beasts of divers sorts, and great flocks of turkey, quails, pigeons and partridges; many great lakes abounding with fish, fowl, beavers, and otters.

TEXT: Hilton, William. William Hinton to his Cousin, November 1621. In Chronicles of the Pilgrim Fathers of the Colony of Plymouth, from 1602-1625, collected by Alexander Young. Boston: C. C. Little and J. Brown, 1841.

The sea affords us great plenty of all excellent sorts of sea-fish, as the rivers and isles doth variety of wild fowl of most useful sorts. Mines we find, to our thinking; but neither the goodness nor quality we know. Better grain cannot be than the Indian corn, if we will plant it upon as good ground as a man need desire. We are all freeholders; the rent-day doth not trouble us; and all those good blessings we have, of which and what we list in their seasons for taking.

Our company are, for most part, very religious, honest people; the word of God sincerely taught us every Sabbath; so that I know not any thing a contented mind can here want. I desire your friendly care to send my wife and children to me, where I wish all the friends I have in England; and so I rest

Your loving kinsman,

William Hilton

From Alexander Young's *Chronicles of the Pilgrim Fathers of the Colony of Plymouth, from 1602–1625*. Boston: Charles C. Little and James Brown, 1841.

2 Find Evidence

Reread the statement "We are all freeholders." What is a context clue for the meaning of the word "freeholder"? Why does being a freeholder mean so much to Hilton?

Underline the details that illustrate why this new status is important to Hilton. How does this help you understand why some people made the long and dangerous journey to settle New England?

3 Make Connections

Talk Could a letter like Hilton's have inspired others in England to move to North America? Would it have persuaded you to make such a long journey?

Explore Main Idea and Details

The **main idea** of a text is what the author most wants readers to know about the topic. The author uses **key details** to support the main idea. Sometimes the main idea is stated in the text, but readers often must infer the main idea from the key details.

To find the main idea and key details:

1. Read the text all the way through.

This will help you understand what the text is about.

2. Look at section titles.

These can be clues to how the text is organized and can help you understand what each section is mostly about.

3. Reread the first and last paragraphs in each section.

These paragraphs may state the main idea or give you clues about what the main idea is.

4. Identify key details.

Look for important information, facts, or evidence that seem to support the main idea.

 Based on the text you just read, work with your class to complete the chart below.

Detail
The main idea is that the land they were in was a great place to settle. **Main Idea**

Investigate!

Read pages 140–151 in your Research Companion. Use your investigative skills to look for text evidence that tells you key details and the main idea. Think about the challenges facing the Native Americans and the English settlers in New England.

Detail

Detail

Detail

Main Idea

Think About It

Review your research. Based on the information you have gathered, what do you think were the two greatest challenges facing New England settlers and Native Americans?

Write About It

Write and Cite Evidence

Write an informative essay about the two greatest challenges facing the New England settlers and Native Americans. Use facts and details from the text to support your response.

_____

_____

_____

_____

_____

_____

_____

_____

_____

_____

_____

_____

_____

_____

_____

_____

_____

Talk About It

COLLABORATE

Explain Your Thinking

Tell a partner about your essay. Did you write about the same issues? Do you agree with what your partner chose?

History

Connect to the EQ

ESSENTIAL QUESTION

Make Connections

How did the goals of the Pilgrims and the Puritans in settling North America influence future settlers?

_____

_____

_____

_____

_____

_____

_____

_____

_____

_____

ESSENTIAL EQ QUESTION

Inquiry Project Notes

_____

_____

_____

_____

_____

What Shaped Life in the Middle Colonies?

Lesson Outcomes

What Am I Learning?

In this lesson, you're going to use your investigative skills to learn about life in the Middle Colonies—New York, New Jersey, Pennsylvania, and Delaware.

Why Am I Learning It?

Reading and talking about the Middle Colonies will help you better understand colonial times and how the past still affects life in the area today.

How Will I Know That I Learned It?

You will be able to describe important characteristics of the Middle Colonies, the people who lived there, the way they lived, and the similarities and differences between the colonies.

Talk About It

COLLABORATE

Look at the Details What positive qualities does the painting convey about William Penn and his treaty?

Artist Benjamin West created this painting, *William Penn's Treaty with the Indians*, almost 100 years after the event.

1 Inspect

Read the text from the primary source and the sentences that introduce it. What does the word *autobiography* in the source's title suggest about its content?

- **Circle** words you don't know.
- **Underline** clues that tell you *whom* the text is about, *what* that person did, and *where* and *when* that person did it.
- **Discuss** with a partner what the text shows you about Benjamin Franklin.

My Notes

_____

_____

_____

_____

_____

_____

_____

Young Ben Franklin Arrives in Philadelphia

Benjamin Franklin grew up in Boston, where he was an apprentice in his brother's print shop. Then he argued with his brother when things he wrote got his brother's newspaper in trouble with authorities. So Franklin, who was just seventeen, left Boston for Philadelphia. On the next page is his account of his arrival in Philadelphia in 1723.

THE

PRIVATE LIFE

OF THE LATE

BENJAMIN FRANKLIN, LL.D.

LATE MINISTER PLENIPOTENTIARY FROM THE UNITED
STATES OF AMERICA TO FRANCE, &c. &c. &c.

Originally written by Himself,
AND NOW TRANSLATED FROM THE FRENCH.

TO WHICH ARE ADDED,

SOME ACCOUNT OF HIS PUBLIC LIFE, A VARIETY OF
ANECDOTES CONCERNING HIM, BY M. M. BRISSOT,
CONDORCET, ROCHEFOUCAULT, LE ROY, &c. &c.

AND THE EULOGIUM OF M. FAUCHET,
CONSTITUTIONAL BISHOP OF THE DEPARTMENT OF CALVADOS,
AND A MEMBER OF THE NATIONAL CONVENTION.

LONDON:
PRINTED FOR J. PARSONS, NO. 21, PATER-NOSTER ROW.
1793.

A printed page from Benjamin Franklin's autobiography

In Their Words... Benjamin Franklin

Then I walked up the street, gazing about till near the market-house I met a boy with bread. I had made many a meal on bread, and, inquiring where he got it, I went immediately to the baker's he directed me to, in Second Street, and asked for biscuit, intending such as we had in Boston; but they, it seems, were not made in Philadelphia. Then I asked for a three-penny loaf, and was told they had none such. So not considering or knowing the difference of money, and the greater cheapness nor the names of his bread, I bade him give me three-penny worth of any sort. He gave me, accordingly, three great puffy rolls. I was surprised at the quantity, but took it, and, having no room in my pockets, walked off with a roll under each arm, and eating the other. . . .

Thus refreshed, I walked again up the street, which by this time had many clean-dressed people in it, who were all walking the same way. I joined them, and thereby was led into the great meeting-house of the Quakers near the market. I sat down among them, and, after looking round awhile and hearing nothing said, being very drowsy thro' labor and want of rest the preceding night, I fell fast asleep, and continued so till the meeting broke up, when one was kind enough to rouse me.
This was, therefore, the first house I was in, or slept in, in Philadelphia.

—from *The Autobiography of Benjamin Franklin*

2 Find Evidence

Reread the text from Franklin's autobiography. What first impression does Philadelphia make on Ben Franklin? Cite details to support your answer.

3 Make Connections

Talk Discuss with a partner the things you learn about colonial Philadelphia from reading the text from Franklin's autobiography.

COLLABORATE

Inquiry Tools

Explore Compare and Contrast

You can better understand the ideas in a text if you compare and contrast the details the author provides.

1. **Read the text once all the way through.**

   This will help you understand what the text is about.

2. **Look at the section titles to see how the text is organized.**

   Do the titles offer any clues about which important qualities or characteristics are discussed in the text?

3. **Think about what the author wants you to know.**

   When you **compare** two things, you tell how they are the same. When you **contrast** things, you tell how they are different. Consider what the author wants you to know about similarities and differences between colonial Philadelphia and Boston.

4. **Find specific similarities and differences.**

   While reading, ask yourself in what specific ways colonial Philadelphia and Boston were alike. Then ask yourself in what specific ways they were different.

Based on the primary source you just read, work as a class to compare Philadelphia and Boston. List one similarity and one difference in the Venn diagram below.

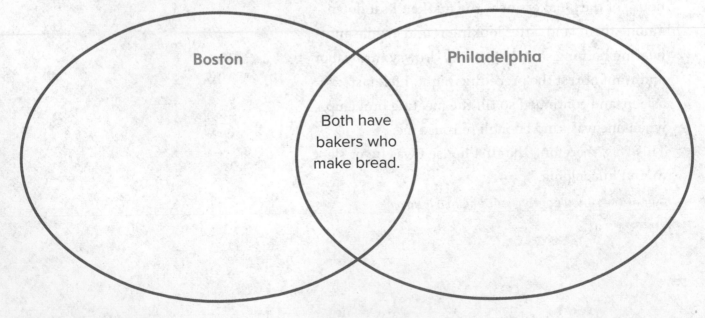

Boston   Philadelphia

Both have bakers who make bread.

Copyright © McGraw-Hill Education

114 Lesson 4 What Shaped Life in the Middle Colonies?

U.S. History
Making A New Nation
RESEARCH COMPANION

Investigate!

Read pages 152–163. Then add details to the Venn diagram about the similarities and differences between the New York and Pennsylvania colonies. Add at least five similarities and six differences (three for each colony).

Comparing and Contrasting New York and Pennsylvania

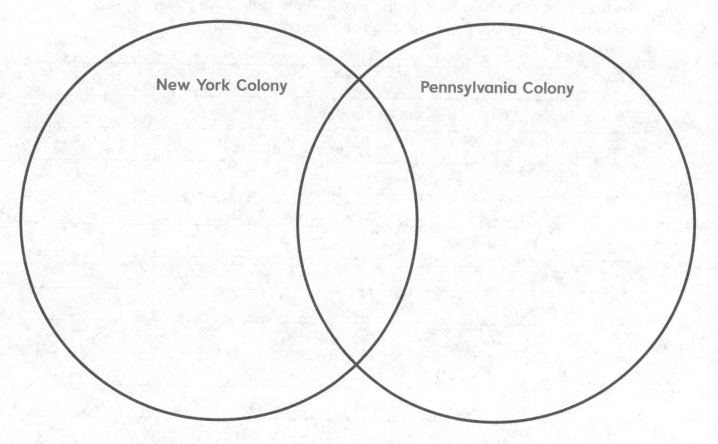

New York Colony

Pennsylvania Colony

Think About It

Review your research. Based on the information you have gathered, how was life in Pennsylvania similar to life in New York? How was it different?

Write About It

Write an Essay

Would you rather be a Quaker settler in the Pennsylvania colony or an English settler in the New York colony? Explain your preference, supporting your opinions with facts and details from the text.

_____

_____

_____

_____

_____

_____

_____

_____

_____

_____

_____

_____

_____

_____

_____

_____

_____

Talk About It

COLLABORATE

Defend Your Claim

Work with a partner who preferred to live in a different colony. Discuss the reasons for your preference. Did your partner make any good points that might change your mind?

Connect to the ESSENTIAL EQ QUESTION

Consider Cause and Effect

Think about the diversity of ethnic backgrounds, religions, and economic opportunities in the Middle Colonies. How did the diversity affect life in these colonies?

_____

_____

_____

_____

_____

_____

_____

_____

ESSENTIAL EQ QUESTION Inquiry Project Notes

_____

_____

_____

_____

_____

How Did Economics Impact People in the Southern Colonies?

Lesson Outcomes

What Am I Learning?

In this lesson, you're going to use your investigative skills to explore how economics of the Southern Colonies shaped people's lives.

Why Am I Learning It?

Reading and talking about the lives of people in the Southern Colonies will help you understand how economics shaped their lives.

How Will I Know That I Learned It?

You will be able to summarize and describe the economics of the Southern Colonies, explain how this agricultural economy led to the rise of slavery, and support your explanation with facts and details from the text.

Talk About It

COLLABORATE

Look at the Details What does this cross-section of a British slave ship tell you about the conditions of the passage from Africa to the Americas for captured Africans?

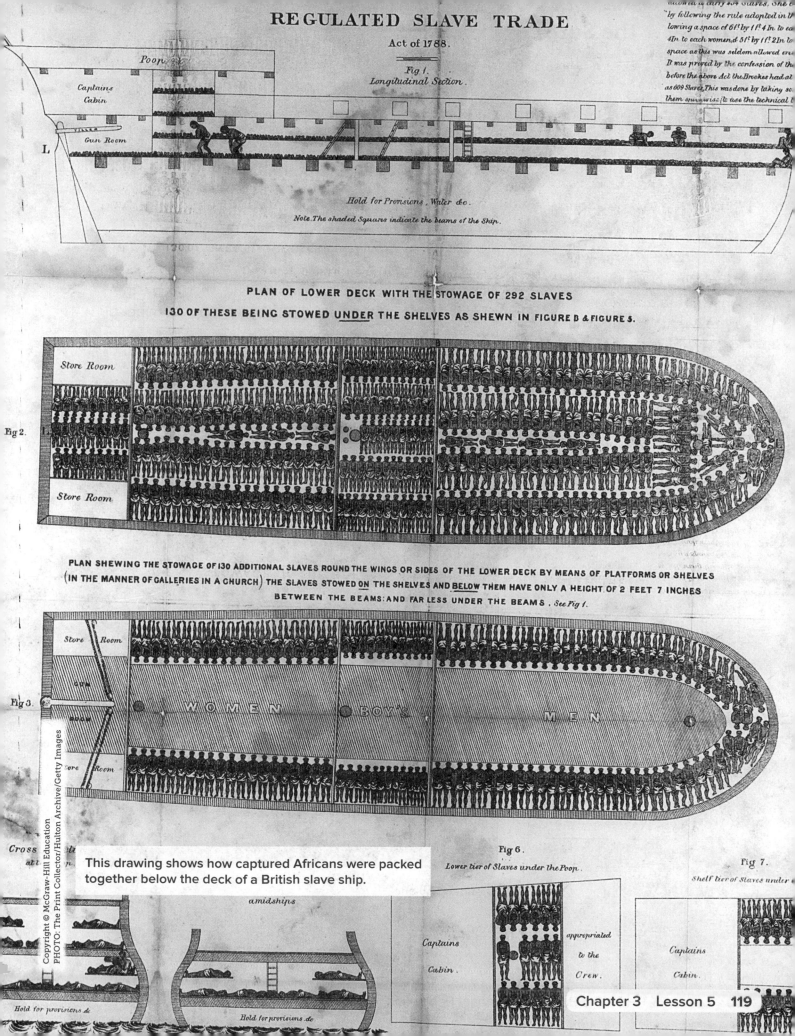

REGULATED SLAVE TRADE

Act of 1788.

Fig. 1.
Longitudinal Section.

Poop.

Captains Cabin.

Gun Room

TILLER

L

Hold for Provisions, Water &c.

Note. The shaded Squares indicate the beams of the Ship.

PLAN OF LOWER DECK WITH THE STOWAGE OF 292 SLAVES
130 OF THESE BEING STOWED UNDER THE SHELVES AS SHEWN IN FIGURE 0 & FIGURE 5.

Fig 2.

Store Room

Store Room

PLAN SHEWING THE STOWAGE OF 130 ADDITIONAL SLAVES ROUND THE WINGS OR SIDES OF THE LOWER DECK BY MEANS OF PLATFORMS OR SHELVES
(IN THE MANNER OF GALLERIES IN A CHURCH) THE SLAVES STOWED ON THE SHELVES AND BELOW THEM HAVE ONLY A HEIGHT OF 2 FEET 7 INCHES
BETWEEN THE BEAMS: AND FAR LESS UNDER THE BEAMS. See Fig 1.

Fig 3.

Store Room

GUN ROOM

Store Room

WOMEN   BOY'S   MEN

Cross

at

amidships

Fig 6.
Lower tier of Slaves under the Poop.

Fig 7.
Shelf tier of Slaves under

Captains Cabin.

appropriated to the Crew.

Captains Cabin.

Hold for provisions &c.

Hold for provisions &c.

This drawing shows how captured Africans were packed together below the deck of a British slave ship.

1 Inspect

Read Look at the title. What will the text be about?

- **Circle** words you don't know.
- **Underline** clues that help answer the questions Who, What, Where, When, or Why.
- **Discuss** with a partner what you know about slavery in colonial America.

My Notes

_____

_____

_____

_____

_____

_____

_____

_____

_____

_____

_____

Olaudah Equiano's Account of Enslaved Life

One of the most detailed accounts of life as an enslaved person was written by Olaudah Equiano in the 1700s. His autobiography provides important information about the slave trade and the experiences of enslaved people. Equiano wrote that he was born in West Africa, in what is now the nation of Benin. When he was 11, slave traders kidnapped him. His account of traveling from Africa to the West Indies on a slave ship is a horrifying description of the brutal treatment of enslaved people. In the following excerpt, Equiano describes an experience on a Virginia plantation.

Olaudah Equiano

In Their Words... Olaudah Equiano

I was a few weeks weeding grass, and gathering stones in a plantation; and at last all my companions were distributed different ways, and only myself was left. I was now exceedingly miserable, and thought myself worse off than any of the rest of my companions; for they could talk to each other, but I had no person to speak to that I could understand. In this state, I was constantly grieving and pining, and wishing for death rather than anything else. While I was in this plantation, the gentleman, to whom I suppose the estate belonged, being unwell, I was one day sent for to his dwelling-house to fan him; when I came into the room where he was I was very much affrighted at some things I saw, and the more so as I had seen a black woman slave as I came through the house, who was cooking the dinner, and the poor creature was cruelly loaded with various kinds of iron machines; she had one particularly on her head, which locked her mouth so fast that she could scarcely speak and could not eat nor drink. I was much astonished and shocked at this contrivance, which I afterwards learned was called the iron muzzle. Soon after I had a fan put in my hand, to fan the gentleman while he slept; and so l did indeed with great fear.

— from *The Interesting Narrative of the Life of Olaudah Equiano, or Gustavus Vass, the African*

2 Find Evidence

Reread In the Primary Source quotation, Olaudah Equiano indicates he was frightened as he was fanning the slave owner. Why do you think this was?

Reread the statement "at last all my companions were distributed different ways, and only myself was left." What does the word *distributed* mean? Name a word that has the same meaning as *distributed*.

3 Make Connections

Write Think about what Olaudah Equiano describes in the Primary Source quotation. Then write a paragraph explaining why you think the colonists would force other human beings to live in the kinds of circumstances described.

COLLABORATE

Explore Cause and Effect

Some of the events you will read about in this lesson have cause-and-effect relationships. To better understand history, it is important to know about cause and effect. The **causes** of historical events explain why things happened, and the **effects** of the events show why the events are important to people afterwards.

1. Look for transitional words related to causes and effects.

Because, therefore, as a result, in order to, and similar transitional words and phrases can indicate cause-and-effect relationships.

2. Take note of chronology.

Texts will often present cause-and-effect relationships in the order that they happen. This is not always true, though, so be careful.

3. Analyze the events.

Would an event have happened without this particular cause? Would the effect have been the same if the earlier event had never happened? Ask yourself questions like these to determine how strong the relationship between two events is.

4. Note that an event may have more than one cause or effect.

There are usually multiple causes for a historical event. Similarly, a historical event may impact many future events.

Based on the text you just read, work with your class to complete the chart below.

Cause		Effect
Equiano saw an enslaved woman wearing an iron muzzle.	→	

Investigate!

Read pages 164–175 in your Research Companion. Use your investigative skills to identify events and circumstances that led to the growth of slavery in the Southern Colonies.

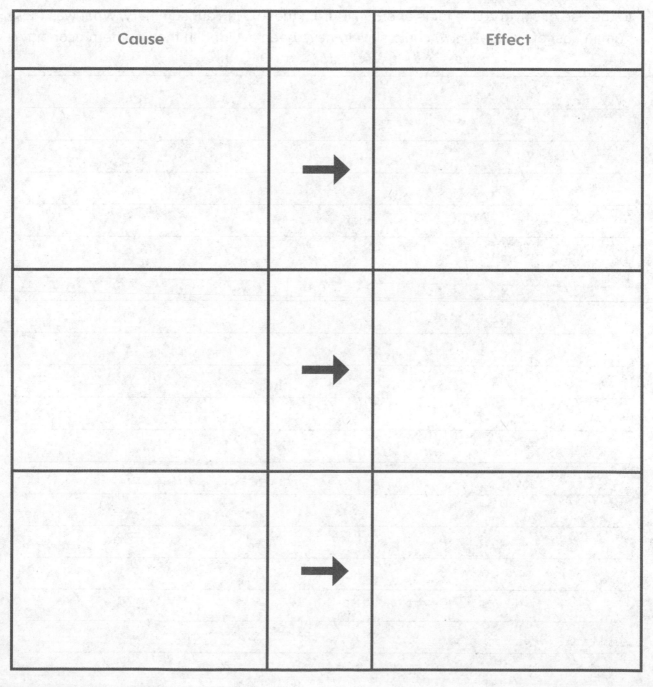

Cause		Effect
	→	
	→	
	→	

Think About It

Review your research. Based on the information you have gathered, how did the way of life in the Southern Colonies lead to the rise of slavery?

Write About It

Explain What Happened

In your own words, write a summary of how the economy of the Southern Colonies led to the rise of slavery. Use facts and details from the text in your summary. What was the human cost of slavery? How could slavery have been avoided in the Southern economy?

_____

_____

_____

_____

_____

_____

_____

_____

_____

_____

_____

_____

_____

_____

_____

_____

_____

_____

Talk About It

Share Your Thinking

Exchange summaries with a partner. Compare and contrast your explanations of how the agricultural economy of the Southern Colonies led to slavery. What did your partner include that you did not?

History

Connect to the EQ

Pull It Together

What positive and negative effects did European settlements have on North America and the people living there?

_____

_____

_____

_____

_____

_____

_____

_____

_____

EQ Inquiry Project Notes

_____

_____

_____

_____

_____

What Is the Impact of People Settling in a New Place?

Inquiry Project

Explain the Impact . . .

For this project, you will write a short narrative that illustrates the relations between a specific group of European settlers and the Native Americans they encountered.

Complete Your Project

Use the checklist below to evaluate your project. If you left anything out, now's your chance to fix it!

☐ Check that your narrative reflects the settlers and Native Americans you researched.

☐ Ensure that you describe events from the point of view of both sides, using effective dialogue and descriptions.

☐ Identify the effects of those relations on the Native Americans' way of life as well as the benefits or setbacks the Europeans experienced.

☐ Support the information in your narrative with strong evidence.

☐ Practice reading the narrative aloud. If your narrative has roles for you and group members, practice as a group.

Share Your Project

Present your narrative to a partner, group, or the class as a whole. Highlight evidence from your research to support your conclusions about how the European settlers and Native Americans affected each other. Take and respond to questions. Explain that you will research any questions you cannot answer.

Reflect on Your Project

Think about the work you did in this chapter and on your project. Use the questions below to help guide your thoughts.

1. How did you choose your European settlers and Native American group?

_____

2. How did you conduct your research? Is there anything you would do differently next time?

_____

_____

3. How did you make sure that your sources were reliable?

_____

Chapter Connections

Use pictures, words, or both to reflect on what you learned in this chapter.

The most interesting thing I learned:

Something I learned from a classmate:

A connection I can make with my own life:

Why Is the **Western Hemisphere** So Diverse?

Sharing Cultures

Prior to the Age of Exploration, a diverse group of native peoples inhabited what is now North and South America. When explorers set sail looking for new countries and goods, the exchange of cultures accelerated with differing impacts on peoples both native and new. Now, you will investigate the impact of diversity today.

Talk About It COLLABORATE

Discuss

Jazz uses rhythmic and structural elements from West African musical traditions, combined with European harmonies and instruments. It features improvising, in which performers create music on the spur of the moment. How do different cultures affect you? What is something you like that reflects diverse cultures coming together?

The legendary jazz musician Louis Armstrong

Investigate!

Read about culture in the Western Hemisphere on pages 180–183 in your Research Companion. As you read, think about the question: **Why Is the Western Hemisphere So Diverse?**

Think About It

Think about key cultural characteristics—such as language, religion, art, music, or traditions—of where you live in the United States and other countries in the Western Hemisphere. How do diverse groups of people influence different cultures?

Write About It

Write and Cite Evidence

Write about a favorite cultural aspect of where you live. Then tell what countries or peoples influenced this part of your culture. Finally, describe a different country's culture you want to learn more about.

Favorite cultural aspect of where I live:

_____

_____

_____

Who influenced this part of my culture:

_____

_____

_____

Culture I want to learn more about:

_____

_____

_____

Talk About It
COLLABORATE

Compare and Contrast

Compare your writing about culture and diversity with a classmate. Discuss how diverse groups of people from the past and present affected the culture of where you live.

This Is What I Believe

CHARACTERS

Narrator	General Court Judge 1	Mary Williams
Anne Hutchinson	General Court Judge 2	James Madsen
Governor John Winthrop	General Court Judge 3	Townspeople

Narrator: In 1634, when Anne Hutchinson and her family arrived in Boston, a Puritan woman's jobs were to raise children, take care of the household, and obey her husband. Anne Hutchinson, however, believed that she should be allowed to preach to other Puritans. She also believed that Puritanism was too strict.

As the local midwife, she became popular with many women. A group of them often came to hear Anne preach and discuss the Bible with them. Soon, men were coming to these meetings too. Before long, however, male church leaders learned about what Anne was doing. After she refused to stop preaching, they held a trial to decide what to do with her.

(The scene opens on a courtroom. The crowd is noisy. The men sit on one side of the room, and the women sit on the other side. Three judges—the general court—oversee the hearing. Anne Hutchinson sits in a chair by herself. Governor Winthrop stands to quiet the crowd.)

Governor John Winthrop: Order! Order in the court! *(The crowd quiets down.)*

Judge 1: We are here today to hear the case of this woman, Anne Marbury Hutchinson.

Judge 2: She is accused of heresy.

Judge 3: First, we will hear from Mary Williams, a follower of Hutchinson. Mrs. Williams, please take the stand.

(Mary Williams *rises and stands next to the judges.*)

John Winthrop: Mrs. Williams, you have been a member of Mrs. Hutchinson's congregation, haven't you?

Mary Williams: Yes, Governor Winthrop. After Anne helped with my baby, we got to talking about this and that.

Before long, we were discussing the church and how women don't have much of a voice in it, even though we have plenty of good ideas.

Winthrop: *(getting agitated)* And during this time, were you reminded of the teachings of our religion? Of the sacred covenant you signed with the church?

Williams: Well, yes, of course, sir. But what Anne said about women voicing their opinions and their beliefs made sense, sir! It's not fair that all the rules should be handed down by men, and we womenfolk are just expected to follow!

(The crowd grows very noisy; this is a shocking statement.)

Winthrop: Silence! *(The noise quiets.)* Mrs. Williams, your actions have been thoughtless, and you have set a bad example. Sit down, please, madam!

(Mary Williams *sits down. A few other women near her lean over to talk to her; some pat her on the back.*)

Judge 1: The court will now hear from James Madsen, who also attended Mrs. Hutchinson's meetings. Mr. Madsen!

(James Madsen *gets up and takes his place next to the judges.*)

Judge 2: Mr. Madsen, is it true that you allowed yourself to be *preached to by a woman?* What do you have to say for yourself, sir?

James Madsen: Yes, sir. Mrs. Hutchinson and I had a long talk while she helped nurse my boy Jamie, sir. We talked about how all the morals and rules that are placed upon us are not needed to keep us in God's good graces. Really, our salvation comes from that grace alone, and not from all this hard work we Puritans put ourselves through.

(*The crowd grows noisy again; this is a very serious statement against a major belief of the Puritans.*)

Winthrop: Mr. Madsen! Do you realize what you have just said, sir? These statements are heresy! For a woman, who is often guided by emotion, to believe this babble is one thing. But you—you are a man, sir! You have no excuse!

(Winthrop *is overcome with anger and disbelief. He sits down, appearing to be thinking very hard.*)

Judge 3: Mr. Madsen, you can sit down. (Madsen *sits down again.*) Our last witness will be Mrs. Anne Hutchinson herself. Madam, this court is giving you the opportunity to defend yourself against these serious accusations. We recommend that you carefully consider what you say.

(Anne Hutchinson *rises from her chair and stands next to the judges.*)

Anne Hutchinson: Your honors, thank you for allowing me the opportunity to speak to you today. But for my defense, I'm afraid that I have none. What Mary and James have said is true.

I stand by my beliefs and my opinions. Ever since I was a little girl, my father taught me to speak my mind. I have read and studied the Bible in great detail. I cannot find any reason women should not be allowed to preach to a whole congregation—including to men. I cannot find reasons for some of our stricter laws and rules.

Judge 2: Mrs. Hutchinson, what you are saying is heresy. If you do not retract your statements, this court will have to act. I am afraid, madam, that you will not like the consequences.

Judge 1: Yes! Remember your place!

Anne Hutchinson: *(calmly)* I understand. But to be untrue to myself would be heresy as well, for my ideas come from God. I have had a revelation, and God has shown me that I am right to be called as a preacher. I will not show myself to be cowardly simply to avoid punishment.

I will not change my statement. You must do as you think best.

(The crowd is in disbelief. The noise rises again.)

Winthrop: SILENCE! *(All noise stops.)* This woman dares to commit heresy! She dares to think that she has the right to lead the souls of men and women. She makes the false claim that her desire to preach comes directly from God!

Anne Hutchinson, your sins are mighty indeed. This court sentences you to banishment from the Massachusetts Bay Colony. You and your family and followers must leave and never, ever come back. This court is adjourned!

(Anne Hutchinson walks out with her head up, smiling to those around her. Mary Williams and James Madsen follow her. The rest of the crowd is still chattering in disbelief.)

Narrator: Yes, Anne Hutchinson and her family and followers had to leave their homes because of Anne's beliefs. However, they simply decided to make a new start. They founded a town in what is now the state of Rhode Island. There, they were able to worship according to their own beliefs.

Write About It

Write your own play about Anne Hutchinson, Mary Williams, and James Madsen taking place one year after the trial. In the play, you should convey through dialogue and narration what life is like for Anne and her followers in their new Rhode Island colony. Do additional research on the colony to make your play more convincing and interesting.

The Road to War

Why Would a Nation Want to Become Independent?

In this chapter, you'll read about what led to the American colonists' wanting independence from Great Britain. You'll examine several causes that led to war, and you'll understand the motivations and opinions of important groups of people.

Talk About It

Discuss with a partner what questions you have about why the American colonies wanted to be independent from Great Britain. As you research, look for answers to your questions. Let's get started!

Inquiry Project

Which Side Will You Choose?

Write an essay from the perspective of a Patriot, Loyalist, African American, or Native American, outlining his or her reasons for wanting or not wanting a war with Britain. Use evidence from the chapter and outside research. Form small groups that contain multiple perspectives. The group will debate whether the colonies should go to war. Then hold a vote and present your conclusions to the class.

Project Checklist

- ☐ **Choose** to take the perspective of a group discussed in the chapter.

- ☐ **Research** and gather information from reliable sources.

- ☐ **Use** your research to write an essay from the perspective of a member of that group.

- ☐ **Debate** the question of independence and take a vote on what you should do.

- ☐ **Discuss** the outcome of your debate and your election with the class.

My Research Plan

Write down any research questions you have that will help you plan your project. You can add questions as you carry out your research.

_____

_____

_____

_____

_____

Explore Words

Complete this chapter's Word Rater. Write notes
as you learn more about each word.

boycott
My Notes
- ☐ Know It!
- ☐ Heard It!
- ☐ Don't Know It!

habitat
My Notes
- ☐ Know It!
- ☐ Heard It!
- ☐ Don't Know It!

imposing
My Notes
- ☐ Know It!
- ☐ Heard It!
- ☐ Don't Know It!

monopoly
My Notes
- ☐ Know It!
- ☐ Heard It!
- ☐ Don't Know It!

musket
My Notes
- ☐ Know It!
- ☐ Heard It!
- ☐ Don't Know It!

outpost

My Notes

☐ Know It!

☐ Heard It! _____

☐ Don't Know It! _____

_____

recession

My Notes

☐ Know It! _____

☐ Heard It! _____

☐ Don't Know It!

_____

reconcile

My Notes

☐ Know It! _____

☐ Heard It! _____

☐ Don't Know It! _____

repeal

My Notes

☐ Know It! _____

☐ Heard It! _____

☐ Don't Know It! _____

vandalism

My Notes

☐ Know It! _____

☐ Heard It! _____

☐ Don't Know It! _____

Lesson 1

What Caused the Conflict Between Great Britain, France, and Native Americans?

Lesson Outcomes

What Am I Learning?

In this lesson, you're going to use your investigative skills to examine the different goals of the British, the French, and the Native American groups in their conflict over North America.

Why Am I Learning It?

Reading and talking about these goals will help you understand how they contributed to the development and outcome of the French and Indian War.

How Will I Know That I Learned It?

You will be able to identify the differences between these goals, make a claim about how these differences influenced the development and outcome of the French and Indian War, and support your opinion with evidence.

Talk About It

COLLABORATE

Look at the Details This is a portrait of George Washington. What details do you see in this painting and what do you think they say about Washington and his life?

George Washington (circa 1779-1781) by Charles Willson Peale

Why Were the Iroquois Important to the British?

1 Inspect

Read Look at the title "Why Were the Iroquois Important to the British?" Which word in the title signals that the text will describe cause and effect?

- **Circle** words that you don't know.
- **Underline** words that give reasons.
- **Discuss** with a partner the reasons why the Iroquois were important to the British.

My Notes

The Iroquois were a powerful confederacy of five (later six) Native American groups whose homeland was in what is now the state of New York. During the 1600s and early 1700s, the Iroquois dominated the Northeast and Great Lakes regions. Because of this strength, the Iroquois were very important to the British in the French and Indian War. As a result, the British government gave a colonial official, Sir William Johnson, the job of keeping friendly relations between the Iroquois and British settlers.

The Iroquois became British allies because of French policy. When French settlers arrived in North America, they decided to aid the Algonquin and Huron in their struggles with their traditional enemy, the Iroquois. One effect of this policy was that the French strengthened their control over the fur trade. Another effect was that the Iroquois sided with the British against Britain's enemy, France.

PRIMARY SOURCE

In Their Words...
Sir William Johnson

Such was the prowess of the Five Nations' Confederacy, that had they been properly supported by us, they would have long since put a period to the Colony of Canada, which alone they were near effecting in the year 1688. Since that time, they have admitted the Tuscaroras from the Southward, beyond Oneida, and they have ever since formed part of the Confederacy.

—from a letter to the British Board of Trade, November 13, 1763

Onondaga warriors and British soldiers around a council fire in the 1700s

2 Find Evidence

Reread What did Sir William Johnson mean by the "prowess" of the Iroquois? Why did this quality make them important to the British?

What policy did Johnson want the British government to adopt toward the Iroquois? What effect did he expect from this policy?

3 Make Connections

Talk Discuss with a partner why France's policy toward the Native Americans both helped and hurt the French.

Explore Cause and Effect

A *cause* is a reason why something happens. An outcome or result is called an *effect*. Identifying cause-and-effect relationships will help you understand historical events.

1. **Read the text once, all the way through.**

   This will help you understand what the text is about.

2. **Look for words and phrases that signal cause-and-effect relationships.**

   Such signal words and phrases include *cause, effect, because, so, caused, resulted, as a result,* and *due to.*

3. **Identify the events that are linked by such signal words.**

   Be sure you have correctly identified which event is the cause and which is the effect.

4. **Be aware that a cause can have more than one effect, and an effect can have more than one cause.**

   Notice any cases in which more than one cause or effect is indicated.

 Based on the text you just read, work with your class to complete the chart below. Use the text you just read.

Cause	Effect
Sir William Johnson stays on friendly terms with Iroquois. →	

Investigate!

Read pages 192–201 in your Research Companion. Use your investigative skills to identify cause-and-effect relationships among the events of the French and Indian War. Use the chart to organize the information.

Cause

Effect

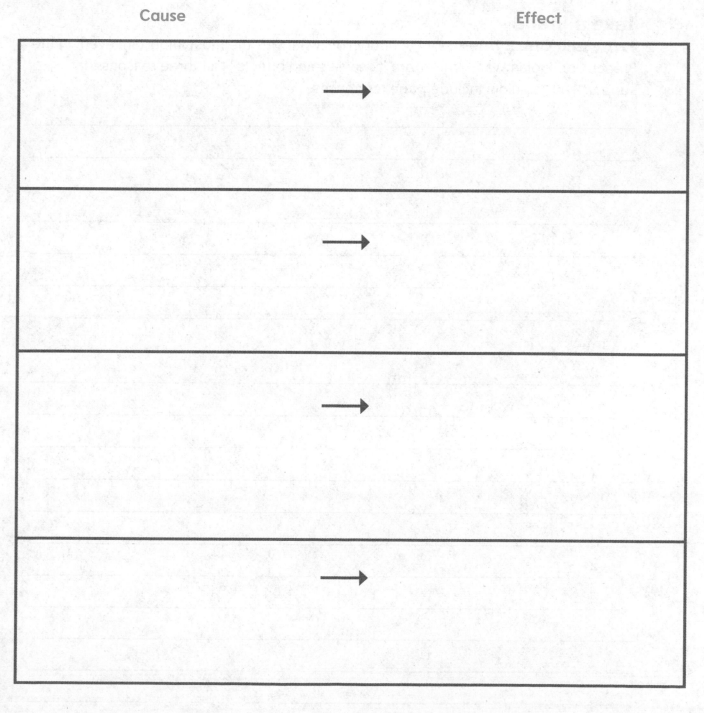

Think About It

Review your research. Based on the information you have gathered, which event do you think was the most important cause of the conflict between the British, the French, and the Native Americans?

Write About It

Take a Stand

Write and Cite Evidence In your opinion, what was the most important event in the French and Indian War? What were its causes and effects? List three reasons that support your opinion. Include page references.

_____

_____

_____

_____

_____

_____

_____

_____

_____

_____

_____

_____

_____

_____

_____

_____

Talk About It

Defend Your Claim

Talk to a classmate who chose a different event from the war. Take turns discussing your opinions and reasons. Do you agree or disagree with your partner's opinion?

Citizenship

Connect to the

Pull It Together

Think about what you have learned about the experiences of the American colonists before, during, and after the French and Indian War. How might these experiences have begun to change how they viewed themselves as citizens?

_____

_____

_____

_____

_____

_____

_____

_____

 Inquiry Project Notes

_____

_____

_____

_____

What Were the Views of the Patriots, the Loyalists, and the British?

Lesson Outcomes

What Am I Learning?

In this lesson, you're going to use your investigative skills to explore British tax policies and the views of the Patriots, the Loyalists, and the British.

Why Am I Learning It?

Reading and talking about these events will help you understand economic and political issues that led to the American Revolution.

How Will I Know That I Learned It?

You will be able to identify the arguments and reasoning of Patriots, Loyalists, and the British, choose one side to defend, and support your argument with evidence from the text.

Talk About It

Look at the Details Examine the two political cartoons on page 147. Which cartoon shows the perspective of the British? Which one shows the colonists' perspective?

Two political cartoons from the era, "The Horse America Throwing his Master" (top) and "The Repeal or the Funeral of Miss Ame-Stamp" (bottom)

1 Inspect

Read Look at the title. What does the title suggest the passage will be about?

- **Circle** any unfamiliar words.
- **Underline** clues about what led to the Stamp Act and what happened after the act was passed.
- **Discuss** with a partner why Edmund Burke criticized the way Parliament ruled the colonies.

My Notes

_____

_____

_____

_____

_____

_____

_____

_____

_____

_____

_____

Edmund Burke Blames Parliament

After the French and Indian War, Great Britain struggled with debt. To help pay for it, King George III and British leaders decided to raise taxes on the colonies. They argued that the colonists should help pay for the troops sent to protect them during the war. In 1765, the British government passed the Stamp Act. It was one of several laws that caused outrage in the colonies.

The Stamp Act required colonists to buy stamps and place them on all printed documents, from newspapers to playing cards. Colonists immediately protested. They called the act unlawful and argued that only elected colonial officials had the power to tax goods.

Colonists were not the only critics of the Stamp Act. A respected member of Parliament, Edmund Burke, spoke on the issue several times before Parliament. He argued that the act was passed in poor judgment. He criticized the British government's strict colonial laws and its refusal to work cooperatively with the colonies. Britain could not just ignore the colonists' complaints, Burke argued. Although he believed that Parliament had the right to tax the colonists, Burke felt that this authority should be used only as a last resort.

In Their Words... Edmund Burke

Never was so critical a measure pursued with so little provision against its necessary consequences. As if all common prudence had abandoned the ministers, and as if they meant to plunge themselves and us headlong into that gulf which stood gaping before them, by giving a year's notice of the project of their stamp act, they allowed time for all the discontents of that country to fester and come to a head, and for all the arrangements which factious men could make towards an opposition to the law.

—from "Observations on a Late State of the Nation," 1769

Edmund Burke speaking before the British Parliament

2 Find Evidence

Reread Note the words "never," "so little," and "abandoned." What do they reveal about Edmund Burke's attitude toward Parliament?

Reread this part of the second sentence: "as if they meant to plunge themselves and us headlong into that gulf which stood gaping before them." What image does Burke create by referring to a gaping gulf and using the word *fester*?

3 Make Connections

Write Summarize Edmund Burke's key reasons for blaming Parliament for unrest in the colonies.

Explore Point of View

A person's point of view is his or her opinion on a topic. Determining point of view can help you understand a person's choices and actions.

1. Identify opinion words.

Which words indicate that someone's opinion is being conveyed? Which words express positive or negative emotions?

2. Look for reasons and evidence.

What reasoning and supporting details can you find that support his or her point of view?

3. Identify actions and choices.

What important decisions or actions does the person make?

4. Evaluate actions for point of view.

Ask yourself, did this person's point of view impact his or her actions?

 Based on the text you just read, work with your class to fill in the details that support Edmund Burke's point of view in the center oval.

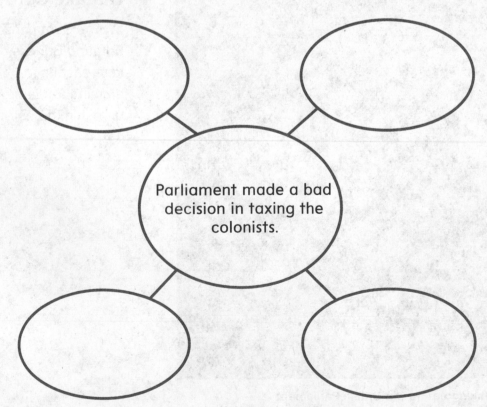

Parliament made a bad decision in taxing the colonists.

Investigate!

Read pages 202–209 in your Research Companion. Use your investigative skills to determine the point of view of the Patriots, the Loyalists, or the British. Use the organizer to track key details that support this point of view.

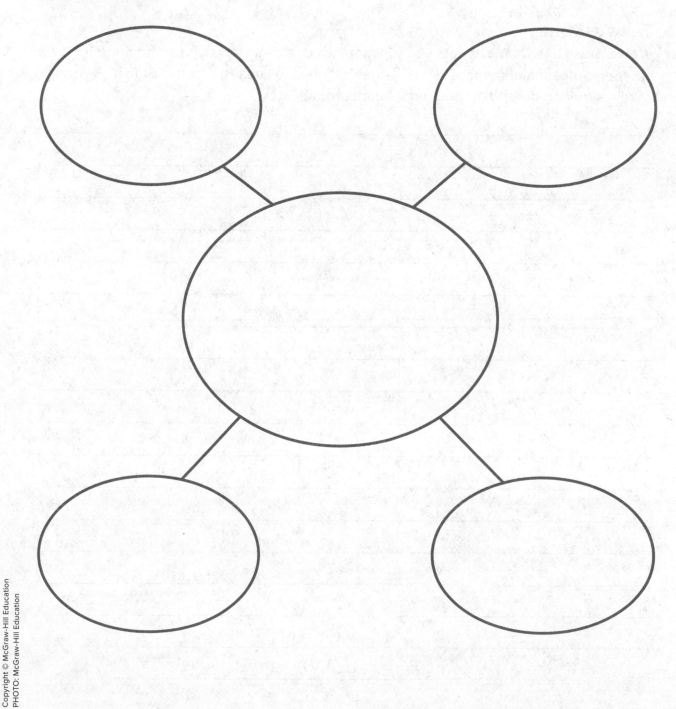

Think About It

Review your research. Based on the information you have gathered, why did some colonists want to stay unified with Great Britain? Why did others want independence?

Write About It

Take a Stand

Write and Cite Evidence In your opinion, which side's views on taxation and independence make the most sense—the Patriots, the Loyalists, or the British? Take a side and defend it, using information from the text.

_____

_____

_____

_____

_____

_____

_____

_____

_____

_____

_____

_____

_____

_____

_____

Talk About It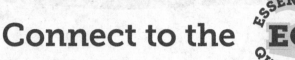

Defend Your Claim

Choose a partner who took a different side. Discuss your reasoning.
Did your partner make any good points that changed your mind?

History

Connect to the ESSENTIAL EQ QUESTION

Pull It Together

Why was it so dangerous for Patriots to act on their wishes to have self-government?
Why did Great Britain feel the need to keep its hold on the colonies?

_____

_____

_____

_____

_____

_____

_____

_____

 Inquiry Project Notes

_____

_____

_____

_____

What Increased Tensions Between Great Britain and the Colonists?

Lesson Outcomes

What Am I Learning?
In this lesson, you're going to use your investigative skills to explore events that led to the American Revolution.

Why Am I Learning It?
Reading and talking about these events will help you understand the reasons that many colonists wanted to break free from Great Britain.

How Will I Know That I Learned It?
You will be able to identify the sequence of events that led to the American Revolution, choose the most important event you believe led to the war, and support your analysis with evidence.

Talk About It
COLLABORATE

Look at the Details What are the differences between the way the British soldiers are portrayed and the way the colonists are portrayed? How do those differences show Revere's point of view of the event?

The BLOODY MASSACRE perpetrated in King—t Street BOSTON on March 5th 1770 by a party of the 29th

BUTCHER'S HALL

Engrav'd Printed & Sold by PAUL REVERE BOSTON

ppyBoston! fee thy Sons deplore,
allow'd Walks befmear'd with guiltlefs Gore
faithlefs P—n and his favage Bands,
murd'rous Rancour ftretch their bloody Hands;
fierce Barbarians grinning o'er their Prey;
rove the Ca—

If fealding drops fromRage from Anguifh Wrung
If fpeechlefs Sorrows lab'ring for a Tongue
Orif aweeping World can ought appeafe
The plaintive Ghofts of Victims fuch as thefe;
The Patriot's copious Tears for each are fhed,
—balms the Dead

But know FATE fummons to that awfu
Where JUSTICE ftrips the Murd'rer of h
Should venal C—ts the fcandal of th
Snatch the relentlefs Villain from her
Keen Execrations on this Plate inf
Shall reach a JUDGE who never can b

The Bloody Massacre in King-Street by Paul Revere shows
the Boston Massacre from the colonists' point of view.

c unhap

ERICK, JAM CALDWELL, CRISPUS ATTUCKS & PA

Killed Six wounded; two of them (CHRISTR MONK & JOHN CLARK) Mortally

Publifhed in 1770 by Paul Revere

Read Look at the title of the time line. What does it tell you about what happens next in American history?

- **Circle** Parliament's actions.
- **Underline** the colonists' actions.
- **Discuss** with a partner the cause-and-effect relationship between Parliament's actions and the colonists' actions.

My Notes

_____

_____

_____

_____

_____

_____

_____

_____

_____

_____

_____

The Events That Led to the Boston Massacre

April 5, 1764 – The Sugar Act

To pay Britain's war debt, Parliament passes the Sugar Act. The act places a colonial tax on imported sugar and molasses. Previous sugar taxes were not enforced. Starting in 1764, colonists who do not pay the tax on sugar products are to be fined and arrested. The colonists stage protests.

March 22, 1765 – The Stamp Act

Parliament passes the Stamp Act, requiring colonists to purchase a stamp for all paper documents, such as newspaper and letters. The money collected from the sale of stamps goes directly to Great Britain, not the colonial government. Colonial protests increase.

May 15, 1765 – The Quartering Act

The Quartering Act is also passed. This requires colonial governments to pay for the housing of British troops and allows the British government to force colonists to let soldiers live on their property, if necessary. No similar law existed in Britain. Colonists call the act unfair.

October 7–25, 1765 – The Stamp Act Congress

Representatives from nine colonies form the Stamp Act Congress. They determine that, since colonists cannot vote in Parliamentary elections, Parliament has no right to tax them. They call for a boycott of British goods.

March 18, 1766 – The Declaratory Act

Parliament declares that it has the right to tax the colonies, but it also repeals the Stamp Act.

June 29, 1767 – The Townshend Acts

Parliament passes The Townshend Acts, adding a tax on goods that are imported from Great Britain. These goods include tea, glass, paper, lead, and paint. Colonists organize another boycott.

August 1, 1768 – The Non-Importation Agreement

Boston merchants declare an official boycott of British goods. They formally refuse to purchase or sell imported tea, paper, glass, or paint until the Townshend Acts are repealed.

October 1, 1768 – The Arrival of More British Troops

Parliament sends more British soldiers to Boston to deal with the growing political unrest in the city.

March 5, 1770 – The Boston Massacre

A group of colonists begins to insult a squad of British soldiers and throws snowballs at them. The soldiers fire into the crowd. Five colonists are killed.

2 Find Evidence

Reread Note the year of the first event in the time line. Then look at the year of the last event in the time line. How many years do these events span?

Then reread the events in the time line. Why is it important that so much happened within a short span of time? What does that tell you about the relationship between the colonists and Great Britain at this time in history?

3 Make Connections

Talk Discuss with a partner the patterns of behavior in the time line. What did the colonists usually do in response to Parliament? When did they change their behavior? Why?

Explore Chronology

Thinking about chronology, or the order in which things happen, will help you make connections between related events.

1. Read the text all the way through.

This will help you understand how the text is organized.

2. Look at section titles.

This will give you clues about which events are significant.

3. Watch for specific dates and signal words.

Pay attention to dates and signal words as you read. Words and phrases such as *first, then, within a few months*, and a *few years later* signal the order in which events happen.

4. Find key facts about each event.

As you read about each event, think about what the key facts and details suggest about the growing tensions between the colonists and Great Britain.

Based on the text you just read, work with your class to complete the chart below.

Event	Date	Key Facts
The Sugar Act		

U.S. History
Making A New Nation
RESEARCH COMPANION

Investigate!

Read pages 210–215 in your Research Companion. Use your investigative skills to identify the sequence of events that led to the American Revolution. Consider how each event is a reaction to another event.

Event	Date	Key Fact

Event	Date	Key Fact

Event	Date	Key Fact

Think About It

Review your research. Based on the information you gathered, what was the most important event that led to war with Great Britain?

Write About It

Take a Stand

Write and Cite Evidence Write an opinion essay about the most important event that led to war with Great Britain. What events led up to this moment? What happened as a result of it? Use facts and details from the text to support your opinion.

_____

_____

_____

_____

_____

_____

_____

_____

_____

_____

_____

_____

_____

_____

Talk About It

Defend Your Claim

Choose a partner who wrote about a different event. Discuss the different impacts your events had. Do you agree or disagree with your partner? Why?

History

Connect to the EQ

Pull It Together

How did the growing tension between the colonies and Great Britain eventually lead to war?

_____

_____

_____

_____

_____

_____

_____

_____

_____

 Inquiry Project Notes

_____

_____

_____

_____

ESSENTIAL EQ QUESTION

Why Would a Nation Want to Become Independent?

Inquiry Project

Which Side Will You Choose?

Remember, for this project you will write an essay from the perspective of someone from the colonies outlining his or her reasons why the colonists should or should not go to war. You will then debate the issue in groups.

Complete Your Project

Use the checklist below to evaluate your project. If you left anything out, now's your chance to fix it!

☐ Give three reasons why the person you have chosen would or would not want to go to war with Great Britain.

☐ Form a small group with classmates who have chosen people of a different background or perspective.

☐ Take turns presenting your perspectives on whether or not the colonists should go to war.

☐ As a group, consider why a Patriot's opinion might be different from that of other groups of people at the time.

☐ Take a vote on the issue after the debate.

Share Your Project

Now it's time to present your group's conclusions to the class. Discuss any similarities and differences in your debates. Provide reasons that led to your group's voting for or against going to war. Consider what you have learned from debating the issue. Answer any questions from the class.

Reflect on Your Project

Think about the work you did in this chapter and on your project. Use the questions below to help guide your thoughts.

1. Why did you choose the person that you researched? _____
_____

2. How did you conduct your research? Is there anything you would do

differently next time? _____

_____

3. How did you make sure that your sources were reliable? _____

_____

Chapter Connections

Use pictures, words, or both to reflect on what you learned in this chapter.

The most interesting thing I learned:

Something I learned from a classmate:

A connection I can make with my own life:

Why Do People Pay Taxes?

Stamping Mad

American colonists paid taxes on printed items, sugar, tea, and other British goods. As you have read, disputes over taxes and representation paved the road to war between colonists and the British government. Now, you'll investigate the impact of taxes, spending, and government economic decisions today.

Talk About It

Look at the Details

In 1765, the British Parliament passed the Stamp Act. The act required colonists to pay taxes on every printed piece of paper colonists used, such as newspapers, licenses, and even playing cards. The British government wanted to raise money to pay for defending the colonies. This propaganda ad was created by colonists in response to the Stamp Act. How did the colonists feel about the tax? How do you think people feel about paying taxes today?

Investigate!

Read about taxes and spending, budget debates, and ways the government tries to grow the economy on pages 218–221 in your Research Companion. As you read, think about the question: **Why Do People Pay Taxes?**

Think About It

Review your research. Based on the information you have gathered, what do you think is the most effective use of tax dollars?

Write About It

Take a Stand

Write about one effective use of tax dollars. List three reasons that support your opinion. Include evidence to support your reasons.

Use of Taxes _____

_____

_____

Reasons

1. _____

_____

_____

2. _____

_____

_____

3. _____

_____

_____

Talk About It

COLLABORATE

Defend Your Claim

Talk to a classmate who chose a different use of taxes. Take turns discussing your opinions and supporting evidence. Do you agree or disagree with your partner's opinion. Why?

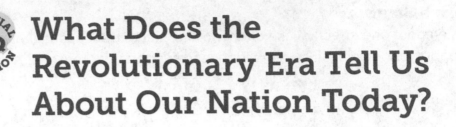

What Does the Revolutionary Era Tell Us About Our Nation Today?

In this chapter, you'll read about the important events and people in the American Revolution. You will think about why these events and people are important, the impact they had on the Revolution, and how the Revolution still affects our nation today. Your explorations will help you answer the Essential Question, and the Inquiry Project will give you an opportunity to pull your ideas together.

Talk About It COLLABORATE

Discuss with a partner what questions you have about the Revolutionary Era. As you research the people, events, and ideas from the Revolutionary Era, look for answers to your questions. Let's get started!

Inquiry Project

How Would Our Lives Have Been Impacted If . . . ?

You and your classmates will research people, ideas, and events that had an impact during the American Revolution. You will each choose one to develop a time line card for. You will evaluate the information in the classroom time line and choose what you think are the five most important people, ideas, or events. Then you will take one item from the time line and consider how our country would be different today if it had never happened.

Project Checklist

- ☐ **List** important events, people, and ideas from the chapter.
- ☐ **Work** as a group to assign a time line card to each class member or to small groups.
- ☐ **Assemble** the class time line.
- ☐ **Choose** what you think are the five most important events on the time line.
- ☐ **Defend** your choices.

My Research Plan

Write down any research questions you have that will help you plan your project. You can add questions as you carry out your research.

_____

_____

_____

_____

_____

Explore Words

Complete this chapter's Word Rater. Write notes as you learn more about each word.

blockade
My Notes
- ☐ Know It!
- ☐ Heard It!
- ☐ Don't Know It!
_____
_____
_____

inflation
My Notes
- ☐ Know It!
- ☐ Heard It!
- ☐ Don't Know It!
_____
_____
_____

mercenary
My Notes
- ☐ Know It!
- ☐ Heard It!
- ☐ Don't Know It!
_____
_____
_____

militia
My Notes
- ☐ Know It!
- ☐ Heard It!
- ☐ Don't Know It!
_____
_____
_____

monarch
My Notes
- ☐ Know It!
- ☐ Heard It!
- ☐ Don't Know It!
_____
_____
_____

negotiate

☐ Know It!

☐ Heard It!

☐ Don't Know It!

My Notes

_____

_____

_____

profiteer

☐ Know It!

☐ Heard It!

☐ Don't Know It!

My Notes

_____

_____

_____

rebel

☐ Know It!

☐ Heard It!

☐ Don't Know It!

My Notes

_____

_____

_____

reconciliation

☐ Know It!

☐ Heard It!

☐ Don't Know It!

My Notes

_____

_____

_____

traitor

☐ Know It!

☐ Heard It!

☐ Don't Know It!

My Notes

_____

_____

_____

Lesson Outcomes

What Am I Learning?

In this lesson, you're going to use your investigative skills to explore events that happened at the beginning of the American Revolution.

Why Am I Learning It?

Reading and talking about these events will help you understand their impact on the American Revolution and our nation today.

How Will I Know That I Learned It?

You will be able to identify the chronology of events at the start of the American Revolution, state an opinion about which event was most important, and support your opinion with evidence.

Talk About It

COLLABORATE

Look at the Details What do you think is happening? How do you know this happened long ago? What do their dress and appearance tell you about these men?

The Battle at Bunker's Hill
drawn by Henry A. Thomas

Patrick Henry Speaks Out

1 Inspect

Read Look at the title. What does "Patrick Henry Speaks Out" suggest about the tone of the text?

- **Circle** words you don't know.
- **Underline** clues that help you answer the questions Who, What, Where, When, or Why.
- **Discuss** with a partner what Patrick Henry thinks the people of Virginia should do and why.

In March of 1775, the House of Burgesses met in Richmond, Virginia, to discuss a solution to painful taxes imposed by the British government. The House of Burgesses was an assembly of elected members who represented the settlements and plantations of Virginia.

Several members pleaded for more time to persuade the British government to repeal, or end, the taxes. Finally, a member named Patrick Henry rose to speak. He mentioned the city of Boston, where there had been conflicts between the colonists and the British. He asked what Virginia could do. He went on to say, "We have done everything that could be done to avert the storm which is now coming on."

The only possible action left, Henry said, was to take up arms and fight. The House of Burgesses then voted to organize a **militia** for Virginia.

My Notes

_____

_____

_____

_____

_____

_____

_____

_____

_____

_____

_____

PRIMARY SOURCE

In Their Words... Patrick Henry

Our brethren are already in the field! Why stand we here idle? What is it that gentlemen wish? What would they have? Is life so dear, or peace so sweet, as to be purchased at the price of chains and slavery? Forbid it, Almighty God! I know not what course others may take; but as for me, give me liberty or give me death!

—from "Speech to the Virginia House of Burgesses," March 23, 1775, Richmond, Virginia

Patrick Henry Addressing the Virginia Assembly

2 Find Evidence

Reread What do you think is the purpose of Patrick Henry's speech? What words does he use that will help accomplish his purpose?

Examine the statement "Our brethren are already in the field! Why stand we here *idle*?" What does the word *idle* mean? Name a word that has the same meaning as *idle*.

3 Make Connections

Talk Discuss with a partner the reasons that Patrick Henry gives for fighting the British.

Connect to Now How did Patrick Henry's speech have an effect on our country today?

Explore Chronology

Identifying the **chronology**, or order in which things happen, in what you read will help you understand how events in history are related.

1. **Read the text once all the way through.**

   This will help you understand what the text is about.

2. **Look at the section titles to see how the text is organized.**

   Do the titles offer any clues as to which important events are discussed in the text?

3. **Watch for specific dates.**

   Are the events described in the text presented in chronological order? It may help to look for sentences that begin with a date—for instance, "On June 18, 1775, . . ."

4. **Find key facts about the events.**

   While reading, ask yourself what key facts about each event show that it was important to the start of the American Revolution.

COLLABORATE

Based on the text you just read, work with your class to complete the chart below.

Event	Date	Key Facts
Patrick Henry's speech to the House of Burgesses		

Investigate!

Read pages 228–237 in your Research Companion. Use your investigative skills to identify the chronology of events at the start of the American Revolution. Use the chart to organize information.

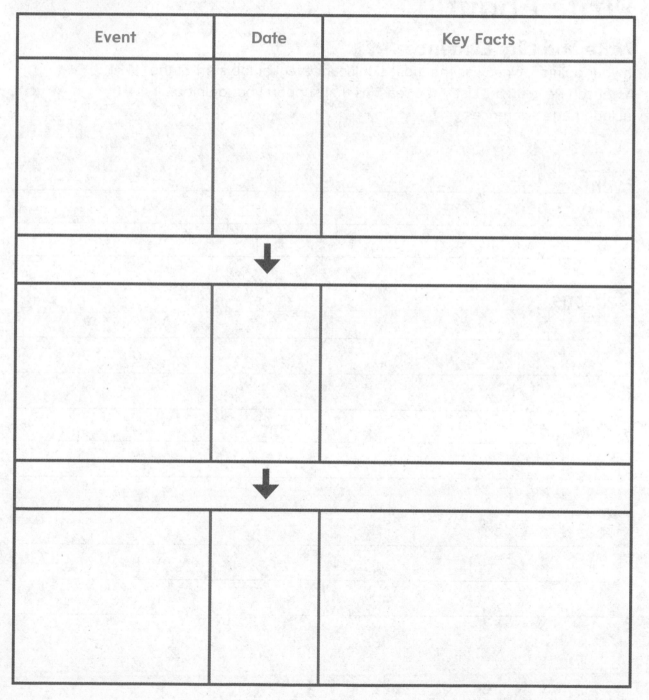

Event	Date	Key Facts
	↓	
	↓	

Think About It

Take a Stand

Review your research. Based on the information you have
gathered, what do you think was the most significant
event at the start of the American Revolution?

Write About It

Write and Cite Evidence

In your opinion, what was the most significant event at the start of the
American Revolution? List three reasons that support your opinion.
Include page references.

Event _____

_____

_____

Reasons

1. _____

_____

_____

2. _____

_____

_____

3. _____

_____

_____

Talk About It

Defend Your Claim

Talk to a classmate who chose a different event. Take turns discussing your opinions and supporting evidence. Do you agree or disagree with your partner's opinion? Why?

History

Connect to the EQ

Pull It Together

Think about the people and events that you read and talked about in this lesson. How did these help shape our nation today?

_____

_____

_____

_____

_____

 Inquiry Project Notes

_____

_____

_____

_____

_____

_____

_____

Why Is the Declaration of Independence Still Important Today?

Lesson Outcomes

What Am I Learning?

In this lesson, you're going to use your investigative skills to learn about the Declaration of Independence and explore why it is still important today.

Why Am I Learning It?

Reading and talking about the Declaration of Independence will help you learn more about what it means and how it affects your life today.

How Will I Know That I Learned It?

You will be able to explain the reasons for important parts of the Declaration of Independence and recognize the ways they still affect the country today.

Talk About It   COLLABORATE

Look at the Details How do you think the members of the Second Continental Congress felt after declaring independence from Great Britain? How do the details in this picture support your answer?

THE REBELS OF '76.

OR, THE FIRST ANNOUNCEMENT OF

THE GREAT DECLARATION.

EXPLANATION.—It is sunset on the 4th of July, 1776. The members of the old Continental Congress, having signed the Declaration, are seen in the act of leaving the Hall of Independence. HANCOCK, distinguished by his dark dress, stands on the steps in front of the hall-door, announcing to a friend that the Declaration has just been signed. FRANKLIN is seen at his right, JEFFERSON leans against the right pillar of the door. ADAMS is conversing with Jefferson—between their heads is seen the face of LIVINGSTON, and against the left pillar stands ROGER SHERMAN. These form the group on the steps. We then commence on the left of the picture, and counting every figure, discover the following persons: 1, a citizen; 2, WILSON, a signer; 3, a citizen; 4, a tory; 5, a signer; 6, a lady; 7, her father; 8, the Indian who bore the Declaration to the camp of Washington; 9, Thomas Paine, talking with No. 10, BENJAMIN RUSH, and 11, ROBERT MORRIS, both signers. Behind them the heads of citizens are seen, and to the right, a crowd of patriots, Quakers, tories, &c. eagerly disputing the nature and merits of the Declaration.

Entered according to act of Congress, in the year 1860, by S. Ashton in the Clerks Office of the District Court of the U. S. for the Eastern District of Pennsylvania.

The Rebels of '76, or the First Announcement of the Great Declaration

1 Inspect

Read Look at the text. What point is the author making?

- **Circle** words you don't know.
- **Underline** clues that help you understand unfamiliar words and concepts.
- **Discuss** with a partner what point the author wants the reader to understand and agree with in this final paragraph.

My Notes

_____

_____

_____

_____

_____

_____

_____

_____

_____

_____

Jefferson's Bold Declaration

In the final paragraph of the Declaration of Independence, Thomas Jefferson made the most important statements in the entire document. These statements represented the creation of a new nation, the United States of America. The colonists were now on a dangerous path from which it would be difficult to turn back.

PRIMARY SOURCE

In Their Words... Thomas Jefferson

We, therefore, the Representatives of the united States of America, in General Congress, Assembled, appealing to the Supreme Judge of the world for the rectitude of our intentions, do, in the Name, and by Authority of the good People of these Colonies, solemnly publish and declare, That these United Colonies are, and of Right ought to be Free and Independent States; that they are Absolved from all Allegiance to the British Crown, and that all political connection between them and the State of Great Britain, is and ought to be totally dissolved; and that as Free and Independent States, they have full Power to levy War, conclude Peace, contract Alliances, establish Commerce, and to do all other Acts and Things which Independent States may of right do.

—from the Declaration of Independence

John Trumbull's painting of the writers of the Declaration of Independence presenting their draft to the Second Continental Congress hangs in the United States Capitol Rotunda.

2 Find Evidence

Reread the statement "Absolved from all Allegiance to the British Crown."

Give an example of a word that means the same thing as *absolved*. Then give a word that means the same as *allegiance*. Then explain what the phrase means.

3 Make Connections

Talk Did the 56 men who signed the Declaration of Independence have the authority to separate the colonies from Great Britain? Why or why not?

Explore Cause and Effect

A **cause** is an event that makes something else happen. An **effect** is an event that happens as a result of a cause. Looking for cause-and-effect relationships can help you better understand what you read.

To find the main idea and key details:

1. **Read the text all the way through.**

   This will help you understand what the text is about.

2. **Watch for specific changes.**

   Ask yourself, "What happened?" The answer to this question helps you identify an effect.

3. **Look for explanations.**

   When you have identified an effect, ask yourself, "Why did this happen?" Knowing why something happened will help you explain its cause.

4. **Look for clue words.**

   Words such as *because, therefore, so*, and *as a result* are clues that signal a cause-and-effect relationship. Recognizing these words will help you answer the question "Why did this happen?"

 Based on the text you just read, work with your class to complete the chart below.

Cause	Effect
The colonies declare that all political connection between the United States and Great Britain is null and void. →	

Investigate!

Read pages 238–247 in your Research Companion. Use your investigative skills to look for text evidence that tells you how important parts of the Declaration of Independence are still important today.

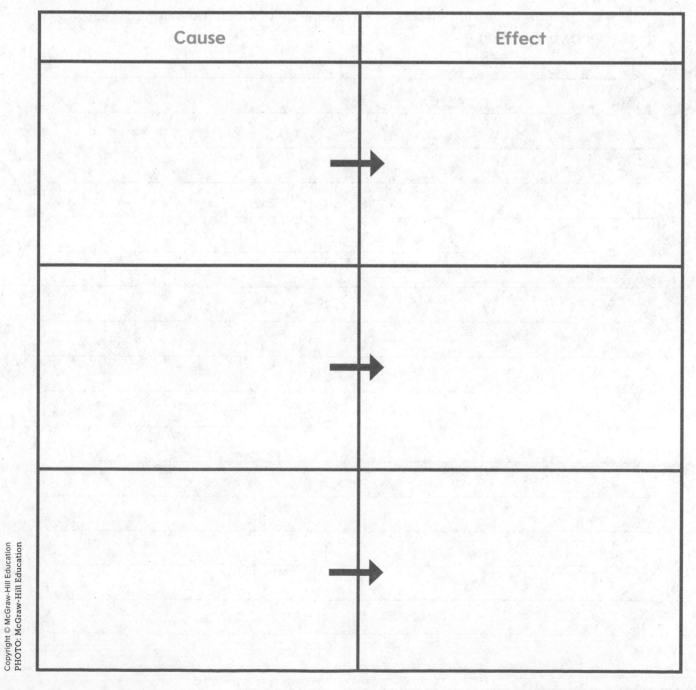

Cause	Effect

Think About It

Review your research. Based on the information you have gathered, what are the important ideas in the Declaration of Independence?

Write About It

Write and Cite Evidence

What was the most important effect of the Declaration of Independence? List reasons that support your opinion.

_____

_____

_____

_____

_____

_____

_____

_____

_____

_____

_____

_____

_____

Talk About It
COLLABORATE

Support Your Thesis

Talk to a classmate who chose a different effect. Take turns discussing your theses and supporting evidence. Do you agree or disagree with your partner's thesis? Why?

Civics

Connect to the

Make Connections

Which key ideas of the Declaration of Independence remain important today?

_____

_____

_____

_____

_____

_____

_____

_____

Inquiry Project Notes

_____

_____

_____

_____

_____

What Were the Defining Moments of the War?

Lesson Outcomes

What Am I Learning?

In this lesson, you're going to use your investigative skills to learn about the defining moments of the Revolutionary War.

Why Am I Learning It?

Reading and talking about the defining moments of the war will help you learn more about how the colonists ultimately won the war.

How Will I Know That I Learned It?

You will be able to make and support inferences about the defining moments of the war.

Talk About It

COLLABORATE

Look at the Details How is Washington shown in this picture? What are his men doing? From the way this portrait was painted, do you think this was an important moment of the war?

Washington Crossing the Delaware
by Emanuel Leutze

Trying Times

From 1776 to 1783, Thomas Paine published a series of sixteen papers called *The American Crisis*. The essays described the conflict with Great Britain as a fight between good and evil.

Paine wrote the first essay in December 1776. During the brutal winter of 1777–1778 at Valley Forge, George Washington ordered that the paper be read aloud to the troops. He hoped that it would inspire them to continue fighting despite the cold, disease, and starvation they faced.

1 Inspect

Read Look at the text. What point is the author making?

- **Circle** words you don't know.
- **Underline** clues that help you understand unfamiliar words and concepts.
- **Discuss** with a partner what the first sentence means: "These are the times that try men's souls." How does that phrase describe what the Revolutionary War was like?

My Notes

_____

_____

_____

_____

_____

_____

_____

_____

_____

_____

_____

_____

PRIMARY SOURCE

In Their Words... Thomas Paine

These are the times that try men's souls. The summer soldier and the sunshine patriot will, in this crisis, shrink from the service of their country; but he that stands it now, deserves the love and thanks of man and woman. Tyranny, like hell, is not easily conquered; yet we have this consolation with us, that the harder the conflict, the more glorious the triumph. What we obtain too cheap, we esteem too lightly: it is dearness only that gives every thing its value.

—from *The American Crisis*, Number 1

American soldiers endured brutal winters during the war.

2 Find Evidence

Reread Examine the statement "the summer soldier and the sunshine patriot will, in the crisis, shrink from the service of their country." What type of people is Paine describing? What other types of people does Paine mention?

Put the phrase "What we obtain too cheap, we esteem too lightly" into your own words. What is Paine saying about the American Revolution with this phrase?

3 Make Connections

Talk What did Paine want to convince the readers of *The American Crisis* to do?

Explore Making Inferences

When you read, you make inferences about the text when the author does not directly state his or her purpose or point. To make a valid inference, you combine **evidence** from the text with what you know from your own experience.

To make an inference:

1. **Read the text all the way through.**

   This will tell you what the text is about.

2. **Reread the text looking for important information—key details, facts, and evidence.**

   Keep track of these clues. They will help you infer.

3. **Ask yourself, What does the text say?**

   Consider the key ideas the author is telling you.

4. **Then ask yourself, What do I already know?**

   Connect something you already know with key ideas you have learned from the text to make an observation.

COLLABORATE Based on the text you just read, work with your class to complete the chart below.

Text Evidence	What I Know	Inference
Washington had *The American Crisis* read to soldiers during their most challenging time.		

Investigate!

Read pages 248–257 in your Research Companion. Use your investigative skills to look for text evidence that tells you about the defining moments of the Revolutionary War and helps you make inferences about those events.

Text Evidence	What I Know	Inference

Think About It

Review your research. Based on the information you have
gathered, why do you think a country as powerful as
Great Britain was unable to stop the colonial forces?

Talk About It

Small-Group Discussions

Create a list of reasons that the colonists were able to turn the tide of the war. Read the
completed list aloud and decide which two reasons are the most important.

_____

_____

_____

_____

_____

_____

_____

_____

_____

_____

_____

_____

_____

_____

Write About It

News Report

Imagine you are a television reporter covering the Revolutionary War. You must write a report on why the colonies were able to turn the tide of the war.

_____

_____

_____

_____

_____

_____

_____

_____

_____

_____

Connect to the

Make Connections

Think about the qualities that helped the American army turn the tide of the war. How do you see those qualities at work in the United States today?

Inquiry Project Notes

_____

_____

_____

_____

What Was It Like to Live During the Revolution?

Lesson Outcomes

What Am I Learning?

In this lesson, you're going to use your investigative skills to learn about what life was like during the American Revolution.

Why Am I Learning It?

Reading and talking about life during the American Revolution will help you understand the hardships people faced.

How Will I Know That I Learned It?

You will be able to explore the motivations and understand the people who lived during the American Revolution.

Talk About It

Find Details Read the text on the next page. What was life like as a soldier during the American Revolution? What would you have done in Joseph Plumb Martin's place?

The Winter at Valley Forge

During the winter of 1777–1778, George Washington's troops camped at Valley Forge in Pennsylvania. The army had great difficulty obtaining enough supplies. Many soldiers became ill, and some died. A Massachusetts private, Joseph Plumb Martin, described his experiences as a soldier in a journal published after the war. The following excerpt describes his time at Valley Forge.

PRIMARY SOURCE

In Their Words...

Joseph Plumb Martin

The men were now exasperated beyond endurance; they could not stand it any longer; they saw no alternative but to starve to death, or break up the army, give up all and go home. This was a hard matter for the soldiers to think upon. They were truly patriotic; they loved their country, and they had already suffered every thing short of death in its cause; and now, after such extreme hardships to give up all, was too much; but to starve to death was too much also. What was to be done? Here was the army starved and naked, and there their country sitting still and expecting the army to do notable things while fainting from sheer starvation.

—from the journal of Joseph Plumb Martin, 1830

1 Inspect

Read Look at the text. What is the poem about?

- **Circle** words you don't know.
- **Underline** clues that help you understand unfamiliar words and concepts.
- **Discuss** why Wheatley wrote the poem. What does it say about her opinions?

My Notes

_____

_____

_____

_____

_____

_____

_____

_____

_____

_____

A Hopeful Poet

Phillis Wheatley was born in Africa. In 1761, at a very young age, she was kidnapped from her family and brought to North America. In Boston, she was purchased by a tailor named John Wheatley, who later freed her. The Wheatleys taught Phillis to read and write, which was an uncommon practice for most slaveholders. She eventually learned Latin and Greek. As a teenager, she began writing poetry. Wheatley composed several of her poems in honor of the new United States. Many of her poems show Wheatley's excitement about the new nation's gaining its independence from Great Britain. That excitement also showed hopefulness for freedom for enslaved people.

Phillis Wheatley

From "To His Excellency General Washington," by Phillis Wheatley

One century scarce perform'd its destined round,
When Gallic[1] powers Columbia's[2] fury found;
And so may you, whoever dares disgrace
The land of freedom's heaven-defended race!
Fix'd are the eyes of nations on the scales,[3]
For in their hopes Columbia's arm prevails.
Anon Britannia[4] droops the pensive head,
While round increase the rising hills of dead.
Ah! Cruel blindness to Columbia's state!
Lament thy thirst of boundless power too late.

Proceed, great chief, with virtue on thy side,
Thy ev'ry action let the Goddess guide.
A crown, a mansion, and a throne that shine,
With gold unfading, WASHINGTON! Be thine.

1 Gallic powers: France

2 Columbia: a female symbol of the United States

3 Fix'd are the eyes of nations on the scales: many nations are interested in the outcome of the war

4 Britannia: a female symbol of Great Britain

2 Find Evidence

Reread Examine the line "Proceed, great chief, with virtue on thy side, / Thy ev'ry action let the Goddess guide."

What evidence tells you Wheatley's opinion of Washington? What other evidence in the poem tells you what Wheatley thinks Washington deserves? How might those things conflict with what Washington himself probably thinks he deserves?

3 Make Connections

Talk What is Wheatley's opinion of Great Britain? How can you tell from the language she uses in the poem?

Explore Motivations

Motivations are the reasons a person does something. When you understand people's motivations for acting a certain way, you learn more about them and the things they did.

1. **Read the text once all the way through.**

   This will help you understand what the text is about.

2. **Ask yourself, Who is this person, and where did he or she come from?**

   Knowing a person's background will help you understand him or her.

3. **Consider how the person's background influenced what happened.**

   The circumstances of a person's life caused that person to make certain decisions or to act a certain way.

4. **Ask yourself, How did this person's motivations influence the event?**

   Look for details about the person's motivations or life circumstances that caused him or her to make a decision or to perform some action.

Based on the text you just read, work with your class to complete the web below by filling out information about a person's background to discover his or her motivation.

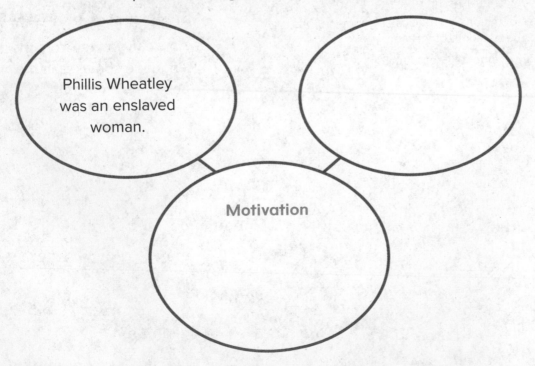

Phillis Wheatley was an enslaved woman.

Motivation

Investigate!

Read pages 258–265 in your Research Companion. Use your investigative skills to look for text evidence that tells you about the motivations of a person from the lesson. Write the person's motivation in the center circle and details that help explain his or her motivation in the surrounding circles.

Think About It

Review your research. Consider what you have learned about life during the American Revolution. What risks did people take by fighting?

Write About It

Write a Letter Create a character set in the Revolution. First, decide the character details: Which side is he or she on? Which group is he or she a part of? What motivates your character? Next, write a letter to a friend or family member from the perspective of your character. Discuss what he or she thinks of the war, how he or she is coping, and what he or she plans to do next.

_____

_____

_____

_____

_____

_____

_____

_____

_____

_____

_____

_____

_____

_____

_____

Talk About It

Interview

Work with a partner. Interview each other. One of you will take the role of a journalist, and the other will be the character you created. The journalist should ask questions such as "Why are you fighting (or not fighting)?" "What do you hope to accomplish?" "How has the war changed your life?" After the first interview, switch roles with your partner.

Connect to the EQ

Make Connections

Think about what you have learned about the American Revolution. What does it have in common with modern conflicts? What is different?

_____

_____

_____

_____

_____

_____

_____

 Inquiry Project Notes

_____

_____

_____

_____

Lesson Outcomes

What Am I Learning?

In this lesson, you're going to use your investigative skills to learn about what Americans gained by winning the war.

Why Am I Learning It?

Reading and talking about what the American colonists gained will help you understand whether the war was worth fighting.

How Will I Know That I Learned It?

You will be able to understand the causes and effects of winning the war.

Talk About It

COLLABORATE

Look at the Details How do you think the soldiers on each side of the drawing feel about what is happening?

SURRENDER OF LORD CORNWALLIS AT YORKTOWN VA. OCT. 19th 1781.

FROM THE ORIGINAL PAINTING BY COLONEL TRUMBULL IN THE CAPITOL AT WASHINGTON

PUBLISHED BY N. CURRIER, 152 NASSAU ST NEW YORK

General Cornwallis surrenders at Yorktown.

Washington's Farewell Orders

1 Inspect

Read Look at the text. What is Washington saying about his men's service in the war?

- **Circle** words you don't know.
- **Underline** clues that help you understand unfamiliar words and concepts.
- **Discuss** the terms that show Washington's opinion.

My Notes

_____

_____

_____

_____

_____

_____

_____

_____

_____

_____

_____

_____

Washington gave these final orders to the troops, believing that he was about to retire after a long career and return to his home, Mount Vernon, Virginia. He thanked the officers and men. He also reminded them of the good work they had done while fighting for independence. Washington wasn't aware at this time that he would later be asked to serve as the nation's first president.

PRIMARY SOURCE

In Their Words...
George Washington

... Let it be known and remembered, that the reputation of the Federal Armies is established beyond the reach of malevolence; and let a consciousness of their achievements and fame still unite the men, who composed them to honorable actions, under the persuasion that the private virtues of economy, prudence, and industry will not be less amiable in civil life than the more splendid qualities of valor, perseverance, and enterprise were in the field.

—from the Farewell Orders to Continental Army, November 2, 1783

Soldiers listen as General George Washington gives his final orders.

2 Find Evidence

Reread Examine the phrase "let it be known and remembered, that the reputation of the federal Armies is established beyond the reach of malevolence."

What does Washington mean when he says that the army's reputation is "beyond the reach of malevolence"? Use a dictionary to help you define any words that are unfamiliar.

Was this a good phrase to include in his farewell orders? Why or why not?

3 Make Connections

Talk What qualities does Washington say he hopes the men will continue to show in their everyday lives?

Explore Cause and Effect

A **cause** is an event that makes something happen. An **effect** is an event that happens as a result of a cause. Looking for cause-and-effect relationships can help you better understand what you read.

To find the causes and effects:

1. **Look for transitions related to causes and effects.**
   Because, therefore, as a result, in order to, and similar transitional words and phrases can indicate cause-and-effect relationships.

2. **Take note of chronology.**
   Texts will often present cause-and-effect relationships in the order that they happen. This is not always true, though, so be careful.

3. **Analyze the events.**
   Ask yourself, would an event have happened without this particular cause? Would the effect have been the same if the earlier event had never happened?

4. **Note that an event may have more than one cause or effect.**
   There are usually multiple causes for a historical event. Similarly, a historical event may impact many future events.

COLLABORATE Based on the text you just read, work with your class to complete the chart below.

Group	Hoped to Gain	Gained or Lost	Results
American soldiers	Hoped for independence from Great Britain		

Investigate!

Read pages 266–275 in your Research Companion. Use your investigative skills to look for text evidence that tells you about what people gained and lost because of their participation in the war.

Group	Hoped to Gain	Gained or Lost	Results

Think About It

Review your research. Recall what you have learned about the people involved in the Revolutionary War. What were their justifications for going to war? Did they succeed in their goals or not?

Write About It

Write a Letter Take the role of a representative of one of the groups involved in the American Revolution. This could be a Patriot, a Loyalist, an African American, a Native American, a member of an ally nation, or even a British soldier. Write a letter to Benjamin Franklin, John Adams, and John Jay about the peace talks in Paris. What conditions would your group like to see included in the peace agreement? Persuade them with specific reasons why your group deserves these conditions.

_____

_____

_____

_____

_____

_____

_____

_____

_____

_____

_____

_____

Talk About It

Defend Your Claims

Discuss as a class who were the real winners and losers of the war.
Who got what they wanted? Who didn't? Who lost the most?
What was fair and what was unfair?

Connect to the EQ

Make Connections

Think about how the American Revolution ended. What lasting
effects did this have on our nation?

_____

_____

_____

_____

_____

_____

_____

 Inquiry Project Notes

_____

_____

_____

_____

_____

_____

ESSENTIAL EQ QUESTION

What Does the Revolutionary Era Tell Us About Our Nation Today?

Inquiry Project

How Would Our Lives Have Been Impacted If...?

Remember that for this project, you and your classmates will design a time line featuring important people, ideas, and events that had an impact during the American Revolution. Choose one to develop a time line card for. After you evaluate the information in the classroom time line, choose what you think are the five most important people, events, or ideas. Take one item from the time line and consider how our country would be different today if it had never happened.

Complete Your Project

Use the checklist below to evaluate your project. If you left anything out, now's your chance to fix it!

☐ Talk about how our nation would be different today if one of the time line events had never happened.

☐ Answer questions from others about points you made.

☐ Support the information about your person, event, or idea with strong evidence.

☐ Clearly communicate information on your time line card.

Share Your Project

When you share your time line card with the class, be sure to prepare and practice a couple of times. Speak loudly and clearly. Look your listeners in the eye. Support your ideas with evidence from your research.

Reflect on Your Project

Think about the work you did in this chapter and on your project. Use the questions below to help guide your thoughts.

1. Why did you choose the person, idea, or event?

_____

2. How did you evaluate your choice? Is there anything you would do

differently next time? _____

_____

3. How did you make sure that your person, idea, or event was significant?

_____

_____

Chapter Connections

Use pictures, words, or both to reflect on what you learned in this chapter.

The most interesting thing I learned:

Something I learned from a classmate:

A connection I can make with my own life:

How Do Citizens Make Their Views Heard?

Active Citizenship

No taxation without representation! This was among the rallying cries of the American Revolution. The American colonists wanted a say in the laws and policies that controlled their lives. Now, Americans must continue to stay active in their government and community to ensure the country lives up to the ideals on which it was founded.

Government officials hear from the people they represent at special meetings called town hall meetings.

Talk About It   COLLABORATE

Discuss

A town hall meeting is one way to speak to a government official. What are the advantages of attending a town hall meeting?

Investigate!

Read about the rights and responsibilities of citizens on pages 278–281 in your Research Companion. As you read, think about the question: **How Do Citizens Make Their Views Heard?**

Think About It

Identify an issue in your school you would like to see changed. Consider who is affected by this issue and why it needs to be changed.

Write About It

Take a Stand

Write an action plan for how you would make a change to an issue in your school. Describe the issue you want to change and at least three steps you could take to address the issue.

Issue: _____

_____

Step 1: _____

_____

Step 2: _____

_____

Step 3: _____

_____

Talk About It

Defend Your Claim

Present your plan to a partner or group. Explain why it will work and consider feedback. How do you think you would be able to convince more people to help work for your plan?

Surviving the Winter at Valley Forge

Narrator	Jonathan *(soldier)*	Grandfather
Mother	Father	
Martha *(sister)*	Lawrence *(brother)*	

Narrator: Our play begins in the cold winter of 1778. We visit the home of the Millers, a Patriot family in Concord, Massachusetts. The Millers' oldest son, Jonathan, is an 18-year-old soldier with the Continental Army at Valley Forge in Pennsylvania, under General George Washington's command. The Millers are worried about Jonathan. They have heard that the soldiers at Valley Forge are exhausted and need food and supplies.

The Millers have just received a letter from Jonathan.

Mother: Come here, everyone! Gather around! I have a letter from Jonathan at Valley Forge!

Martha: Is he safe, Mother?

Mother: Yes, thank goodness! Let us read his letter.

Jonathan *(appears, alone on the opposite side of the stage. He is seated as if writing a letter):*

My Dear Family,

Greetings to you all. I miss you very much, especially you, dear Grandfather! Life here is rather difficult. It has been snowing and raining without end. We sleep in log huts and try to keep warm around the campfires. Many soldiers are ill and some have died.

Do not worry, however, for I remain in good health. I am willing to fight for our freedom at any cost.

General Washington is trying to get us more supplies. He is a great man and our victory is in his hands. He has asked for help from a Prussian general named von Steuben. He is teaching us how to march and work together. We'll be a polished fighting force soon, and I know the Patriots will win!

I hope you are well. Please write to me and send me news. Words from you are a great comfort.

Your soldier son and brother,

Jonathan

(Jonathan exits.)

Mother: My poor, brave boy! So young and such a Patriot!

Martha: How can anyone in these colonies support the king?

Father: It is tradition, I suppose. They are Loyalists because they still consider themselves subjects of the British king.

Grandfather: It can be difficult for people to change. Why, when I was a boy, I would never have dreamed of fighting the king! Such a thing would have been impossible to consider.

Father: We Patriots have a grander vision for the future of the colonies. We want the right to form our own government and make our own laws!

Martha: I've heard that there are people who help the British troops by giving them information, shelter, and supplies! Is that true?

Mother: I am afraid that is so, Martha. They call themselves Loyalists because they are loyal to the British crown. But I believe that we will win the war against Great Britain and gain our freedom!

Lawrence: How can you be certain?

Father: Our army is strong and wants to win.

Lawrence: Yes, but the British army is stronger, and I'm sure they want to win too. They also have the support of a king, while my brother and his fellow soldiers freeze without even blankets and food!

Mother: Yes, Lawrence, but our soldiers know the land well and they are loyal to the cause of freedom. They will fight hard to protect their land and their families.

Grandfather: Yes, my dear. Your reasons are good to remember.

Mother: I still worry for Jonathan. I must send him a woolen shirt and blankets to keep him warm.

Father: And we must also write a letter to Jonathan. He can still receive it before General Washington moves his soldiers again.

Martha: I have the ink and the paper. What shall we say?

Narrator: Winter turned to spring, and conditions began to improve at Valley Forge. Food arrived from local farmers. New soldiers arrived. Baron von Steuben's training began to show in the way the soldiers marched and prepared for battle. The Continental Army had suffered at Valley Forge, but it was ready now to return to the battle for its country's freedom.

Write About It

Write your own play about Jonathan and the other soldiers at Valley Forge. Set the play in the spring of 1778. Jonathan has just received a letter from his family. Have the soldiers talk about their concerns in fighting the British. Jot down your ideas in the space below before writing your play.

_____

_____

_____

_____

_____

_____

_____

Forming a New Government

ESSENTIAL EQ QUESTION

How Does the Constitution Help Us Understand What It Means to Be an American?

In this chapter, you'll read about how the U.S. Constitution was created. You'll learn why the Articles of Confederation was too weak to govern the nation, and you'll learn how the Constitution is evolving to protect the rights of all citizens.

Talk About It COLLABORATE

Discuss with a partner what questions you have about the United States Constitution. As you research, look for answers to your questions. Let's get started!

Inquiry Project

Which Side Will You Choose?

As a class, propose a new amendment to the Constitution that has a good case for and against it. Then, divide into two groups—one in favor of it and one opposed. On a class website, write a series of letters or editorials for and against the amendment, making references to points made in one another's writings.

Project Checklist

☐ **Work together** to choose an amendment that could be argued for or against.

☐ **Research** the history and specifics of the possible amendment topic.

☐ **Use** your research to write a letter or editorial about the amendment.

☐ **Read** the other group's letter, and respond to their claims.

☐ **Develop** a written conversation about the amendment.

My Research Plan

Write down any research questions you have that will help you plan your project. You can add questions as you carry out your research.

_____

_____

_____

_____

_____

Complete this chapter's Word Rater. Write notes as you learn more about each word.

amendment
My Notes

☐ Know It!
☐ Heard It!
☐ Don't Know It!

_____
_____
_____

article
My Notes

☐ Know It!
☐ Heard It!
☐ Don't Know It!

_____
_____
_____

bill
My Notes

☐ Know It!
☐ Heard It!
☐ Don't Know It!

_____
_____
_____

currency
My Notes

☐ Know It!
☐ Heard It!
☐ Don't Know It!

_____
_____
_____

delegate
My Notes

☐ Know It!
☐ Heard It!
☐ Don't Know It!

_____
_____
_____

issue

☐ Know It!

☐ Heard It!

☐ Don't Know It!

My Notes

_____

_____

_____

jury

☐ Know It!

☐ Heard It!

☐ Don't Know It!

My Notes

_____

_____

_____

physical

☐ Know It!

☐ Heard It!

☐ Don't Know It!

My Notes

_____

_____

_____

press

☐ Know It!

☐ Heard It!

☐ Don't Know It!

My Notes

_____

_____

_____

term

☐ Know It!

☐ Heard It!

☐ Don't Know It!

My Notes

_____

_____

_____

What Was the Articles of Confederation and Why Did It Fail?

Lesson Outcomes

What Am I Learning?
In this lesson, you're going to use your investigative skills to explore the Articles of Confederation.

Why Am I Learning It?
Reading and talking about the Articles will help you understand the process that led to the creation of the United States Constitution.

How Will I Know That I Learned It?
You will be able to evaluate the strengths and weaknesses of the first constitutional document of the United States.

Talk About It

COLLABORATE

Look at the Details How is this image of the Articles of Confederation similar to other important documents from U.S. history? In what ways do you think this document differs from government documents written today?

The Articles of Confederation

1 Inspect

Read Look at the title. What can you infer about the author(s) of this text?

- **Circle** words you don't know. Look them up and rewrite each article in simpler language.

- **Underline** action words in the articles. What actions does the Articles of Confederation grant the states and Congress?

- **Discuss** with a partner why the writers of the Articles of Confederation might have decided to separate the document into different articles.

My Notes

_____

_____

_____

_____

_____

_____

_____

_____

_____

Excerpts From the Articles of Confederation

Article II.

Each state retains its sovereignty, freedom, and independence, and every power, jurisdiction, and right, which is not by this Confederation expressly delegated to the United States, in Congress assembled.

Article X.

The Committee of the States, or any nine of them, shall be authorized to execute, in the recess of Congress, such of the powers of Congress as the United States in Congress assembled, by the consent of the nine States, shall from time to time think expedient to vest them with; provided that no power be delegated to the said Committee, for the exercise of which, by the Articles of Confederation, the voice of nine States in the Congress of the United States assembled be requisite.

Article XIII.

All bills of credit emitted, monies borrowed, and debts contracted by, or under the authority of Congress, before the assembling of the United States, in pursuance of the present confederation, shall be deemed and considered as a charge against the United States, for payment and satisfaction whereof the said United States, and the public faith are hereby solemnly pledged.

In Their Words...
Alexander Hamilton

But the confederation itself is defective and requires to be altered. It is neither fit for war nor peace. The idea of an uncontrollable sovereignty in each state over its internal police will defeat the other powers given to Congress and make our union feeble and precarious. There are instances without number where acts necessary for the general good, and which rise out of the powers given to Congress, must interfere with the internal police of the states . . .

—from a letter to James Duane, September 2, 1780·

2 Find Evidence

Reread What weakness of the Articles of Confederation does Alexander Hamilton identify in this letter?

Examine Reread the statement "the idea of an uncontrollable sovereignty in each state over its internal police will defeat the other powers given to Congress and make our union feeble and precarious." Based on this context, what does the word *feeble* mean? Name a word that has the same meaning as *feeble*.

3 Make Connections

Talk Discuss with a partner how the Articles helped set up a central government. Which responsibilities of government did the founders think were most important?

Explore Pros and Cons

Asking questions about what you read will allow you to judge the positive and negative outcomes of historical events.

1. Read the text all the way through.

This is the best way to understand what the text is about.

2. Answer *who*, *what*, *where*, and *when*.

Write down the dates, places, events, and people mentioned in the text.

3. Make inferences about the historical reasons for an event.

Sometimes the author directly explains how and why something happened; other times, you will have to make inferences. Combine your prior knowledge with what you read in the text to understand the context of the events mentioned in the text.

4. Identify positive and negative effects.

Once you've answered questions about a text, you can use the information to list the pros and cons that resulted from the historical events you've read about.

COLLABORATE

Based on the text you just read, work with your class to complete the chart below.

Pros	Cons
The Articles give states much freedom to govern themselves.	

Investigate!

Read pages 290–297 in your Research Companion. Use your investigative skills to identify the pros and cons of the Articles of the Confederation.

Pros	Cons

Think About It

What were the pros and cons of the Articles of the Confederation?

Write About It

Take a Stand

Write and Cite Evidence Write a short summary of the pros and cons of the Articles of Confederation. How did using this document provide the new nation with lessons about governing?

_____

_____

_____

_____

_____

_____

_____

_____

_____

_____

_____

_____

_____

_____

_____

_____

_____

Talk About It

Defend Your Claim

Discuss the Articles of Confederation with a partner. Why is it important to learn about the Founders' mistakes as well as their triumphs?

Civics

Connect to the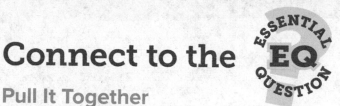

Pull It Together

What would it have meant to the future of the United States if the Articles of Confederation had lasted as the nation's government?

_____

_____

_____

_____

_____

Inquiry Project Notes

_____

_____

_____

_____

_____

_____

Lesson 2

How Does the Constitution Set Up Our Government Framework?

Lesson Outcomes

What Am I Learning?
In this lesson, you're going to use your investigative skills to explore the writing of the U.S. Constitution.

Why Am I Learning It?
Reading and talking about the writing of the Constitution will help you understand our government, its laws, and the ideas behind the laws.

How Will I Know That I Learned It?
You will be able to explain the structure of our government and the reasons for this structure.

Talk About It

Find Details Read the letter from George Washington to the Secretary for Foreign Affairs, John Jay. How do they feel about the Articles of Confederation?

PRIMARY SOURCE

A Letter to John Jay from George Washington, May 18, 1786

I coincide perfectly in sentiment with you, my dear Sir, that there are errors in our national Government which call for correction; loudly, I would add; but I shall find my self happily mistaken if the remedies are at hand. . . . That it is necessary to revise, and amend the articles of Confederation, I entertain no doubt; but what may be the consequences of such an attempt is doubtful. Yet, something must be done, or the fabrick must fall. It certainly is tottering.

—from *The Writings of George Washington*

1 Inspect

Read Look at the two versions of the Preamble to the Constitution.

- **Circle** words you don't know.
- **Underline** phrases that are in both versions.
- **Discuss** in groups of three. Each group member should lead a short discussion for one of the following questions: Why were some things kept? Why were some things removed? Why were some things added?

My Notes

_____

_____

_____

_____

_____

_____

_____

_____

_____

_____

Writing (and Rewriting) the Constitution

The Constitution was not written all at once. It had to be written carefully so that it could cover all of the important laws needed by a national government. On May 25, 1787, fifty-five members of the Constitutional Convention began meeting at Philadelphia's State House to discuss, plan, and write the Constitution.

A first draft was copied and given to the delegates on August 6. They studied and made notes on their copies before making a final draft, signed on September 17, 1787. The Preamble, or introduction, to the Constitution, changed significantly between the two versions. The entire process had taken four months, with only an eleven-day break.

PRIMARY SOURCE

In Their Words...
The Preamble, First Draft

We the People of the States of New-Hampshire, Massachusetts, Rhode-Island and Providence Plantations, Connecticut, New-York, New-Jersey, Pennsylvania, Delaware, Maryland, Virginia, North-Carolina, South-Carolina, and Georgia, do ordain, declare and establish the following Constitution for the Government of Ourselves and our Posterity.

—from the First Draft of the United States Constitution, August 6, 1787

The Constitutional Convention delegates taking turns signing the Constitution

![PRIMARY SOURCE]

In Their Words...

The Preamble, Final Draft

We, the People of the United States, in order to form a more perfect union, establish justice, insure domestic tranquility, provide for the common defence, promote the general welfare, and secure the blessings of liberty to ourselves and our posterity, do ordain and establish this Constitution for the United States of America.

—from the official United States Constitution, September 17, 1787

2 Find Evidence

Reread The Preamble lists five things the government must do: "establish justice, insure domestic tranquility, provide for the common defense, promote the general welfare, and secure the blessings of liberty to ourselves and our posterity, . . ."

Think of an example of how the government does each of these things. Compare your list of examples with lists from other students.

3 Make Connections

Write Imagine you are a delegate at the Constitutional Convention. Is there anything you think should be changed in the second version of the Preamble? Write a short speech explaining what you want added, changed, or removed, and why it is important.

COLLABORATE

Explore Making Inferences

To infer is to find a meaning that is not directly written or spoken. If a bill has trouble getting through Congress, you can infer that many people disagree with it. If a bill gets passed very quickly, on the other hand, then you can infer it was popular among members of Congress. These meanings that we find are called inferences.

When studying history, we often have to infer the reasons for historical persons' decisions, especially if they have not left behind diaries, letters, or other writing explaining their decisions. To make an inference:

1. Read the text closely.

Make sure you understand what is being said.

2. Recall what you know about the topic.

What do you know about the event being described? About the people involved? About what happened before and what came next?

3. Combine what you know with what you have read.

Put the information together to form a more complete picture of what has happened.

COLLABORATE

Based on the text you just read, work with your class to complete the chart below.

What I Know	What I Read	My Inference
	The Preamble highlights several goals for drafting the U.S. Constitution.	

Investigate!

Read pages 298–309 in your Research Companion. Use your investigative skills to infer why some Framers of the Constitution were concerned about either the Virginia Plan's or the New Jersey Plan's structure for a central government.

What I Know	What I Read	My Inference

Think About It

Look back on your research about the difficulties in writing the Constitution. How does the argument over the structure of the legislature illustrate the way the Constitution came to be written?

Write About It

Take a Stand

Write and Cite Evidence Write a dialogue between two delegates at the Constitutional Convention. The dialogue should show the opposing viewpoints in the dispute over the structure of the legislature, which eventually ended in the Great Compromise. In the dialogue, show each delegate's point of view and his reason for thinking that way.

_____

_____

_____

_____

_____

_____

_____

_____

_____

_____

_____

_____

_____

Talk About It

Act It Out

Work with a partner to read aloud or act out each other's dialogues. Afterwards, give your partner feedback. How did your partner illustrate the dispute and compromise?

Civics

Connect to the EQ

Pull It Together

What does the process of writing the Constitution reveal about our system of government?

_____

_____

_____

_____

_____

_____

Inquiry Project Notes

_____

_____

_____

_____

_____

_____

How Do the Constitution and the Bill of Rights Impact Citizens?

Lesson Outcomes

What Am I Learning?

In this lesson, you're going to use your investigative skills to explore how the Constitution and the Bill of Rights affect the people of the United States.

Why Am I Learning It?

Reading and talking about the liberties protected by the Constitution and the Bill of Rights will help you understand our rights.

How Will I Know That I Learned It?

You will be able to summarize how our lives are influenced by the country's founding documents.

Talk About It

COLLABORATE

Find Details Read the quotation from Benjamin Franklin. How did Franklin feel about the Constitution? What "faults" might he be referring to?

In Their Words...
Benjamin Franklin

I agree to this Constitution, with all its faults ... because I think a general Government necessary for us.... I doubt too, whether any other Convention we can obtain, may be able to make a better Constitution....

—Benjamin Franklin at the conclusion of the Constitutional Convention in 1787

Did You Know?

At the time of the Constitutional Convention, Ben Franklin was in his 80s and in poor health. Much of the convention occurred during summer months, and the hot room made Franklin even more uncomfortable. Yet, he played an important role at the convention, helping to calm things down when tempers flared. Franklin had many of his ideas shot down by other delegates. Among these was a belief that the executive branch should be led by a committee and that Congress should consist of only one house, not two. Nonetheless, Franklin supported the final version of the Constitution.

At the conclusion of the convention, Franklin noted to some of his fellow delegates that George Washington's chair had a half-sun on the back. For months, he had thought about the sun as a possible metaphor for the convention, and he told his colleagues he had wondered "whether it was rising or setting. But now at length I have the happiness to know that it is a rising and not a setting sun."

1 Inspect

Read Look at the titles "The Freedoms of Religion and Expression" and "The First Amendment." What connections are there between the two?

- **Circle** words you don't know.

- **Underline** words related to the concept of "The Freedoms of Religion and Expression."

- **Discuss** with a partner why the writers of the Bill of Rights chose the rights of expression and religious freedom to include as the first addition to the Constitution.

My Notes

_____

_____

_____

_____

_____

_____

_____

_____

The Freedoms of Religion and Expression

The First Amendment of the Constitution protects Americans' freedoms of religion and expression. The amendment is intended to prevent the federal government from punishing citizens for what they say or what they believe. Since the writing of the Constitution, the Supreme Court has ruled on many cases concerning the First Amendment.

The Supreme Court has interpreted the First Amendment to grant four basic rights of expression along with freedom of religion, which allows people to worship as they please. Freedom of speech gives people the right to share their ideas openly. Freedom of the press guarantees the right of the media to publish news freely. Freedom of assembly allows U.S. citizens to gather and hold meetings. Freedom of petition grants the right to sign petitions and to protest government policies. The broad freedoms of expression granted by the First Amendment made possible major U.S. protest campaigns such as the women's suffrage movement and the civil rights movement.

PRIMARY SOURCE

The First Amendment

Congress shall make no law respecting an establishment of religion, or prohibiting the free exercise thereof; or abridging the freedom of speech, or of the press; or the right of the people peaceably to assemble, and to petition the Government for a redress of grievances.

The First Amendment gives U.S. citizens the right to express their opinions publicly.

2 Find Evidence

Reread How does the author present the details of the First Amendment?

Examine Underline the transitional words and phrases that the author uses.

3 Make Connections

Draw Work with a partner to draw a chart of the five basic freedoms protected by the First Amendment. In one column, list the name of the freedom. In the next, list the right that it grants U.S. citizens. In the final column, list any exceptions that are not protected by the First Amendment.

COLLABORATE

Connect to Now How does the First Amendment affect the freedoms you enjoy today?

Summarize

When you write a summary, you list the most important details in a text. Your summary will help you remember and think about the structure of a text.

To write a summary:

1. **Read through the text.**

   This will help you determine the main idea of the text.

2. **Reread and jot down notes.**

   Make notes about the people, places, events, and ideas discussed. Make sure to include only details directly from the text, and not your opinions.

3. **List the most important details.**

   Write down the main details in the order that they appear in the text.

4. **Keep your summary brief.**

   Your summary should be shorter than the original text.

 Based on the text you just read, work with your class to complete the chart below.

Details	The First Amendment to the Constitution protects Americans' freedoms of religion and expression.		
Summary			

Investigate!

Read pages 310–319 in your Research Companion. Use your investigative skills to list important details and to write a summary of one section of the text you read.

Details				

Summary	

Think About It

What is the purpose of the Bill of Rights?

Write About It

Give an Example

Illustrate Choose one right protected by the Bill of Rights. Write and illustrate a comic strip that shows that particular amendment in action.

Talk About It

Explain

Work with a partner who chose a different amendment in the Bill of Rights. Read each other's comic strip, and discuss situations from your own lives in which the amendments would provide you with freedoms.

Connect to the EQ

Pull It Together

How does the Bill of Rights help define what it means to be a citizen of the United States?

_____

_____

_____

_____

_____

_____

 Inquiry Project Notes

_____

_____

_____

_____

_____

_____

_____

How Does the Constitution Help Us Understand What It Means to Be an American?

ESSENTIAL EQ QUESTION

Inquiry Project

Which Side Will You Choose?

Remember, for this project you will propose a new amendment to the Constitution as a class, divide into groups for and against it, and then write a series of online letters in favor of or opposed to the new amendment.

Complete Your Project

Use the checklist below to evaluate your project. If you left anything out, now's your chance to fix it!

☐ Choose an amendment that has a good case for and against it.

☐ Write an online letter or editorial that establishes your point of view.

☐ Use research into the history and specifics of the amendment's topic to defend your point of view.

☐ Read the other group's letter for or against the amendment. Respond to their views respectfully in a new letter.

☐ Develop a written conversation about the amendment.

Share Your Project

Present your group's conclusions about the amendment to the whole class. Consider how passing or not passing the amendment will impact the nation. Make note of whether the other group's letters changed your group's thinking. Be respectful of the points of view of your classmates.

Reflect on Your Project

Think about the work you did in this chapter and on your project. Use the questions below to help guide your thoughts.

1. Why did you choose your position on the amendment?

_____

_____

2. How did you conduct your research? Is there anything you would do differently next time? _____

_____

3. How did you make sure that your sources were reliable? _____

_____

Chapter Connections

Use pictures, words, or both to reflect on what you learned in this chapter.

The most interesting thing I learned:

Something I learned from a classmate:

A connection I can make with my own life:

How Does History Shape a Country's Government?

The IMPACT Today

Like with the American Revolution, a country's history can shape what type of government it has. The United States has had the same form of government and same constitution ever since it became independent. Its form of government even survived the long and violent Civil War. Other countries in North and South America have changed forms of government more often. But many have adopted forms of government and constitutions similar to those of the United States.

Talk About It
COLLABORATE

Look at the Photographs

Some governments are elected by the people and have a system of checks and balances. Other governments are run by a single leader, such as a dictator or monarch, who makes most of the decisions. What do you think are some positives and negatives of those kinds of governments?

Democracy is the most common form of government in the Western Hemisphere today. In the past, dictators led many Latin American countries.

Investigate!

Read about the history and government of other Western Hemisphere countries on pages 322–325 in your Research Companion. As you read, think about the question: **How Does History Shape a Country's Government?**

Think About It

Review your research. Based on what you have learned, what are some common and unique features of governments in the Western Hemisphere? Who has the power in different governments? What is the role of citizens in shaping that power?

Write About It

Write and Cite Evidence

Compare and contrast the government of the United States with the government of another Western Hemisphere country you learned about. How are the two governments alike and different? What is the role of citizens in shaping each government? Which government do you think is best?

Country compared with the United States: _____

How the United States government is alike and different:

_____

_____

_____

Role of citizens in each government:

_____

_____

_____

Government I like best:

_____

Talk About It   COLLABORATE

Defend Your Claim

Talk to a classmate about the pros and cons of the governments you compared. Describe what the ideal government would be if you could start a new government.

What Do the Early Years of the United States Reveal About the Character of the Nation?

In this chapter, you'll read about how the nation's first leaders made decisions that shaped the young United States. You'll examine how important inventions made it easier to travel and communicate. You'll read about how the United States expanded westward. In addition, you'll explore the conflicts and compromises over slavery.

Talk About It

Discuss with a partner what questions you have about how the early years of the United States would define the nation's identity. As you research, look for answers to your questions. Let's get started!

Inquiry Project

Create a Museum Gallery

Create a gallery (print or digital) of three paintings that depict the United States during its early years. Write a museum card for each picture by including the title, the name of the artist, the year it was painted, and a brief description of what the painting shows. Discuss as a group how the paintings work together to tell a story about the character and spirit of the United States.

Project Checklist

☐ **Conduct** research to find three paintings that depict the early years of the nation.

☐ **Research** each painting. Determine what you like and dislike about each painting.

☐ **Create** a museum card for each painting with the facts and details from your research.

☐ **Present** each image and its card to the class. Explain why you chose each painting as you tell about its history.

My Research Plan

Write down any research questions you have that will help you plan your project. You can add questions as you carry out your research.

_____

_____

_____

_____

_____

Complete this chapter's Word Rater. Write notes as you learn more about each word.

abolitionist
My Notes

- ☐ **Know It!**
- ☐ **Heard It!**
- ☐ **Don't Know It!**

_____

cede
My Notes

- ☐ **Know It!**
- ☐ **Heard It!**
- ☐ **Don't Know It!**

_____

composition
My Notes

- ☐ **Know It!**
- ☐ **Heard It!**
- ☐ **Don't Know It!**

_____

fugitive
My Notes

- ☐ **Know It!**
- ☐ **Heard It!**
- ☐ **Don't Know It!**

_____

interchangeable
My Notes

- ☐ **Know It!**
- ☐ **Heard It!**
- ☐ **Don't Know It!**

_____

loom

My Notes

- ☐ Know It!
- ☐ Heard It!
- ☐ Don't Know It!

_____

_____

_____

Manifest Destiny

My Notes

- ☐ Know It!
- ☐ Heard It!
- ☐ Don't Know It!

_____

_____

_____

policy

My Notes

- ☐ Know It!
- ☐ Heard It!
- ☐ Don't Know It!

_____

_____

_____

surge

My Notes

- ☐ Know It!
- ☐ Heard It!
- ☐ Don't Know It!

_____

_____

_____

unconstitutional

My Notes

- ☐ Know It!
- ☐ Heard It!
- ☐ Don't Know It!

_____

_____

_____

How Did Early Decisions Shape the Nation?

Lesson Outcomes

What Am I Learning?

In this lesson, you're going to use your investigative skills to learn about important events and government decisions in the early years of the United States.

Why Am I Learning It?

Reading and talking about those early events and decisions will help you understand the direction the nation took and what effects it had on the future.

How Will I Know That I Learned It?

You will be able to describe the causes and effects of important events in the nation's early years as well as the decisions and policies that the nation's early leaders made.

Talk About It

COLLABORATE

Look at the Details What object near the center of this image stands out among all the cannon fire? What is the artist suggesting with this image?

During the War of 1812, the British tried to capture Fort McHenry, just outside of Baltimore, Maryland.

1 Inspect

Read Look at the lyrics of this primary source and the sentences that introduce them.

- **Circle** words you don't know.
- **Underline** clues that tell you *what* event the text is about, *where* and *when* it takes place, and *how* and *why* it is happening.
- **Discuss** with a partner the event that Francis Scott Key witnessed.

My Notes

_____

_____

_____

_____

_____

_____

_____

_____

_____

_____

_____

The Star-Spangled Banner

During the War of 1812, American Francis Scott Key was detained by the British on a ship in Baltimore Harbor. From the ship, he witnessed the British bombardment of Fort McHenry on September 13, 1814. The next morning, he saw the American flag still flying over the fort. He expressed his feelings in a poem that was later set to music. Known as "The Star-Spangled Banner," it eventually became the national anthem of the United States on March 3, 1931.

PRIMARY SOURCE

O say can you see, by the dawn's early light,

What so proudly we hail'd at the twilight's last gleaming,

Whose broad stripes and bright stars through the perilous fight

O'er the ramparts we watch'd were so gallantly streaming?

And the rocket's red glare, the bombs bursting in air,

Gave proof through the night that our flag was still there,

O say does that star-spangled banner yet wave

O'er the land of the free and the home of the brave?

– from "The Star-Spangled Banner" by Francis Scott Key

2 Find Evidence

Reread Look at the lyrics. What item or thing is the opening question about? Which details in the first two sentences make this clear? What is the significance of this item still being there "by the dawn's early light"?

3 Make Connections

Talk Discuss with a partner why the song is called "The Star-Spangled Banner."

Inquiry Tools

Explore Cause and Effect

A **cause** is an event or action that is the reason something happens. An **effect** is the result of a cause. Often, a situation, event, or decision has more than one cause or more than one effect. Consider the causes and effects of government decisions and policies in the early years of the United States.

1. Read the text once all the way through.

This will help you understand what the text is about.

2. Look at the section titles to see how the text is organized.

This will help you find key events, decisions, and policies in the text.

3. Find reasons or explanations.

While reading, ask yourself what specific reasons led to a particular decision or policy.

4. Watch for specific changes.

While reading, also ask yourself what specific changes resulted from a particular decision or policy.

Based on the text you just read, work with your class to complete the chart below.

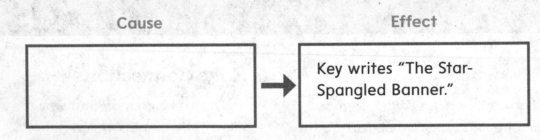

Cause → Effect

Key writes "The Star-Spangled Banner."

Investigate!

Read pages 334–345 in your Research Companion. Use your investigative skills to determine the effects of important decisions made in the early years of the United States. In the "Cause" column, write the decision. In the "Effect" column, describe how the decision impacted the nation.

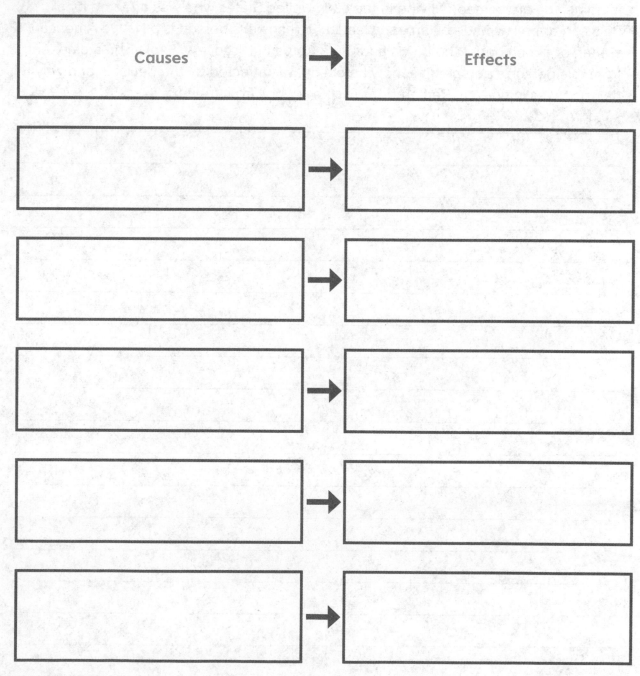

Causes → Effects

Think About It

Review your research. Why was it important to explore the Louisiana Territory?

Write About It

Write a Diary Entry

Imagine you are someone living in the early United States who was affected by a decision or policy made by an early leader. Perhaps this person is a Native American, a settler, or a member of the Lewis and Clark Corps of Discovery. Explain, in a diary entry from this person's perspective, how he or she was affected by the decision and why this decision was important. Remember to use evidence from the text.

Talk About It

Defend Your Claim

Working with a partner, discuss your diary entries. Take turns asking and answering questions that explain who each diary writer is, what that person has been doing, and how one or more government policies or decisions have affected him or her.

History

Connect to the

Consider Cause and Effect

Think about a policy or decision you wrote about in your diary entry. In general, how did it change the nation and its people?

_____

_____

_____

_____

_____

_____

 Inquiry Project Notes

_____

_____

_____

_____

_____

_____

_____

How Did Advancements in Technology and Transportation Shape the Nation?

Lesson Outcomes

What Am I Learning?

In this lesson, you will use your investigative skills to learn about new technology and transportation in the decades after the Revolution and the ways these affected American lives.

Why Am I Learning It?

Reading and talking about new technology and transportation will help you understand their importance in contributing to the growth of the U.S. economy and how they impacted people's lives.

How Will I Know That I Learned It?

You will be able to describe important inventions and other changes and how they addressed problems of travel and communication as well as how they affected the way people worked.

Talk About It

COLLABORATE

Look at the Details How are the different types of boats being powered? How can you tell?

This painting of a river scene shows a flatboat used to transport
goods and several passenger steamboats in the background.

1 Inspect

Read Examine the text of this primary source and the sentences that introduce it.

- **Circle** words you don't know.
- **Underline** details that tell you *what* the steamboat cabin is like, *where* Charles Dickens is going, and *when* he expects to arrive there.
- **Discuss** with a partner the opinions that Dickens seems to have about the steamboat.

My Notes

_____

_____

_____

_____

_____

_____

_____

_____

_____

_____

Charles Dickens Takes an American Steamboat

Britain's Charles Dickens was already a famous writer when he and his wife visited the United States in 1842. After stops on the East Coast, they traveled by canal boat, railroad, and stagecoach to Pittsburgh, Pennsylvania. From there, they took a steamboat called the *Messenger* down the Ohio River to Cincinnati, Ohio. Before the invention of the steamboat, travel by waterway took a long time and relied on the water's current. The following text comes from Dickens's description of that trip.

A caricature of the British author, Charles Dickens

In Their Words... Charles Dickens

The *Messenger* was one among a crowd of high-pressure steamboats, clustered together by a wharf side, which, looked down upon from the rising ground that forms the landing place, and backed by the lofty bank on the opposite side of the river, appeared no larger than so many floating models. She had some forty passengers on board, exclusive of the poorer persons on the lower deck; and in half an hour, or less, proceeded on her way.

We had, for ourselves, a tiny stateroom with two berths in it. . . . It was an unspeakable relief to have any place, no matter how confined, where one could be alone. . . .

We are to be on board the *Messenger* three days: arriving at Cincinnati (barring accidents) on Monday morning. There are three meals a day. Breakfast at seven, dinner at half-past twelve, supper about six. At each, there are a great many small dishes and plates upon the table, with very little in them; so that although there is every appearance of a mighty "spread," there is seldom really more than a joint: except for those who fancy slices of beet-root, shreds of dried beef, complicated entanglements of yellow pickle; maize, Indian corn, apple-sauce, and pumpkin.

—from *American Notes*, Chapter XI

2 Find Evidence

Reread What does the quotation show you about the two kinds of passengers on steamboats? Which kind of passenger is Charles Dickens?

3 Make Connections

Talk Discuss with a partner what you learn about steamboat travel from this primary source.

COLLABORATE

Explore Problem and Solution

Text is often organized by presenting problems and then showing how those problems have been or could be solved.

1. Read the text once all the way through.

This will tell you what the text is about.

2. Look at the section titles to see how the text is organized.

This will help you find key events, decisions, and policies in the text.

3. Find specific problems.

While reading, ask yourself what problems people in the early United States had.

4. Watch for specific solutions.

While reading, also ask yourself which particular inventions or changes offered solutions to those problems.

COLLABORATE Based on the text you just read, work with your class to complete the chart below.

Problem	Solution
Travel by waterway took a long time and was affected by the water's current.	

Investigate!

Read pages 346–353 in your Research Companion. Use your investigative skills to determine how advancements in technology and transportation solved various problems in the early United States. Use the chart below to organize the information.

Problem	Solution

Think About It

In the early 1800s, what was it like to communicate with someone living far away?
Review your research to help you answer.

Write About It

Write an Advertisement

Develop an advertisement aimed at getting people to use one of the new technologies
discussed in this lesson. Encourage those who are wary of the new technology to give it
a try. Support your claims about the new technology with facts and details from the text.
Sketch or describe a graphic to accompany your ad.

_____

_____

_____

_____

_____

_____

_____

_____

_____

_____

_____

_____

_____

_____

_____

_____

Talk About It

Compare Advertisements

Compare your advertisement with a partner's. Which is more likely to persuade people to use the new technology? Why?

Connect to the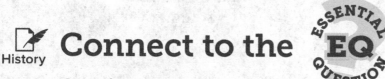

Consider Cause and Effect

How did advances in transportation and communication shape the early United States?

_____

_____

_____

_____

_____

_____

Inquiry Project Notes

_____

_____

_____

_____

_____

_____

_____

Lesson 3

Who Were the People Living in the Early United States?

Lesson Outcomes

What Am I Learning?

In this lesson, you're going to use your investigative skills to explore the various people who lived in the early United States, including the first pioneers, Native Americans, African Americans, and immigrants.

Why Am I Learning It?

Reading and talking about the lives of the people who lived in the early United States will help you understand how people's experiences in the young nation were affected by their race, ethnicity, and gender.

How Will I Know That I Learned It?

You will be able to compare and contrast the experiences of three groups of people who lived in the early United States in a short blog post. Then you will support your findings with facts and details from the text.

Talk About It

Find Details Read the words to "America the Beautiful." What kind of country does the author describe?

O beautiful for spacious skies,

For amber waves of grain,

For purple mountains majesties

Above the fruited plain!

America! America! God shed his grace
on thee,

And crown thy good with brotherhood

From sea to shining sea!

—from "America, the Beautiful"
By Katherine Lee Bates — 1893

"Amber Waves of Grain": A Wheat Field

1 Inspect

Read Look at the title. What do the words "letter to her mother" suggest about the kind of text this will be?

- **Circle** words you don't know.
- **Underline** clues that help you answer the questions *who, what, where, when,* or *why.*
- **Discuss** with a partner how Cathy Greene feels and what her experience as a recent immigrant has been like.

My Notes

Cathy Greene Writes a Letter to Her Mother

Irish immigrants escaping poverty and famine in their own country faced many difficulties once they arrived in the United States. New York City, for example, was very different from the Irish countryside. The environment for many was strange and frightening. In addition, within a very short time, immigrants had to make sure that practical needs were met. They needed to find a place to stay. They needed to find a job in order to support themselves. And then, many experienced the crushing weight of loneliness. They had to leave home; there was very little opportunity there. But they missed home and their families, often intensely.

Cathy Greene, a recent Irish immigrant living in Brooklyn, New York, wrote to her mother in County Kilkenny, Ireland, in 1884, begging her to write her back.

In the mid-1800s, many Irish immigrants came to the United States hoping to escape poverty and starvation.

In Their Words... Cathy Greene

My Dear Mama,

What on earth is the matter with ye all, that none of you would think of writing to me? The fact is I am heart-sick, fretting. I cannot sleep the night and if I chance to sleep I wake with the most frightful dreams.

To think that it's now going and gone into the third month since ye wrote to me. I feel as if I'm dead to the world. I've left the place I was employed. They failed in business. I was out of place all summer and the devil knows how long. This is a world of troubles.

I would battle with the world and would never feel dissatisfied if I would hear often from ye. . . . I know if I don't hear from ye prior to the arrival of this letter . . . I will be almost dead."

—from Cathy Greene's letter to her mother, August 1, 1884

2 Find Evidence

Reread Notice the problems Cathy Greene has to deal with. How do you think these problems affect her anxiety over not hearing from her mother?

Reread the line "I would battle with the world and never feel dissatisfied if I would hear often from ye." What is Cathy Greene trying to tell her mother in these lines?

3 Make Connections

Talk Discuss with a partner the many feelings an immigrant might feel when family members are far away.

COLLABORATE

Explore Compare and Contrast

Comparing and contrasting groups of people in the early United States will help you understand how the experiences of the groups are alike and different.

1. **Read the text all the way through.**

   This will tell you what the text is about.

2. **Look for groups of people whose experiences are described.**

   This will help you decide which groups of people you will compare and contrast.

3. **Choose three groups that you can easily compare and contrast.**

   This will help you analyze the experience of three groups of people.

4. **List the main experiences of each group and how they are similar to or different from the experience of other groups.**

   This will help you find likenesses and differences among the groups.

COLLABORATE
Based on the text you just read, work with your class to describe the experiences of immigrants and to compare them with the experiences of another group you know of.

Group	Experiences	Likenesses/Differences
Immigrants		

Investigate!

Read pages 354–363 in your Research Companion. Use your investigative skills to identify different groups of people and their experiences. Then compare their experiences with those of a different group.

Group	Experiences	Likenesses/Differences

Think About It

How were people's experiences in the early United States different depending on their race, ethnicity, or gender?

Write About It

Write a Blog Post

Choose three groups of people who lived in the young United States. Compare and contrast their experiences in a short blog post. Use facts and details from the text in your comparison-contrast blog.

_____

_____

_____

_____

_____

_____

_____

_____

_____

_____

_____

_____

_____

_____

_____

_____

_____

Talk About It

Share Your Thinking

Exchange your blog post with that of a partner. What likenesses or similarities did your partner include that you did not?

Connect to the

Pull It Together

What were the early years of the United States like for different groups of people?

_____

_____

_____

_____

_____

 Inquiry Project Notes

_____

_____

_____

_____

_____

_____

_____

_____

How Did Westward Expansion Impact People Living in the United States?

Lesson Outcomes

What Am I Learning?

In this lesson, you're going to use your investigative skills to explore westward expansion and how it impacted people's lives in the 1800s.

Why Am I Learning It?

Reading and talking about westward expansion will help you understand its impact on people and the nation.

How Will I Know That I Learned It?

You will be able to identify the point of view of a person or group of people impacted by westward expansion.

Talk About It

COLLABORATE

Look at the Details What does the painting show? What does the title of the painting suggest about the event?

The Trail of Tears by Robert Lindneux

What Is Manifest Destiny?

1 Inspect

View Look at the image. What is the picture showing?

- **Think** about the figures shown in the painting.
- **Examine** clues that help you understand what event each part of the picture shows.
- **Discuss** why you think the artist painted it.

My Notes

_____

_____

_____

_____

_____

_____

_____

_____

_____

_____

_____

_____

_____

In the 1800s, people who struggled on the East Coast found the prospect of settling the open territory of the West appealing. They wanted to make the trip despite the obstacles they would face on the long, slow journey. This drive to settle the West was known as **Manifest Destiny.** It eventually led to the United States stretching from the Atlantic to the Pacific.

Many works of art explore the openness and natural beauty of the West. John Gast's painting *American Progress* shows major advances such as the telegraph, the stagecoach, and the steam engine. This progress is represented by the figure of a woman moving gracefully from the East to the West. The book she is carrying shows that she is bringing along civilization's knowledge.

Opponents of Manifest Destiny pointed out that it ignored the rights of native peoples living in the West and disrespected their ways of life. Many settlers believed that it was God's will for the nation to expand westward. These settlers believed that their way of life and their religion ought to dominate the continent from East to West.

John Gast was a Prussian-born artist who lived in Brooklyn. He was known for allegorical, or symbolic, painting. George Crofutt, the publisher of the era's most popular travel guides, commissioned the painting *American Progress* in 1872 from Gast. This was more than twenty years after the concept of Manifest Destiny was born. Crofutt published the reproductions of the painting in his Western travel guides, where thousands saw the image.

American Progress by John Gast

2 Find Evidence

Look Again Examine the woman at the center of the picture. What is she holding? From which direction does she seem to be coming? Where is she going? Is this a portrait of a real woman? What might she represent?

Examine Read the statement "John Gast's painting *American Progress* shows major advances such as the telegraph, the stagecoach, and the steam engine." Why do you think Gast included these in the painting?

3 Make Connections

Talk Do you think those who saw this painting reprinted in travel guides at the time of westward expansion would have been inspired to travel west? Do you think Native Americans would have been offended by this painting? Why or why not?

Explore Point of View

A person's point of view is his or her opinion on a topic. Determining point of view can help you understand a person's choices and actions.

1. **Identify opinion words.**

   Which words indicate that someone's opinion is being conveyed?

   Which words express positive or negative emotions?

2. **Look for reasons and evidence.**

   What reasoning and supporting details can you find that support his or her point of view?

3. **Identify actions and choices.**

   What important decisions or actions does the person make?

4. **Evaluate actions for point of view.**

   Ask yourself, did this person's point of view impact his or her actions?

Based on the text you just read, work with your class to fill in the details that support John Gast's point of view in the center oval.

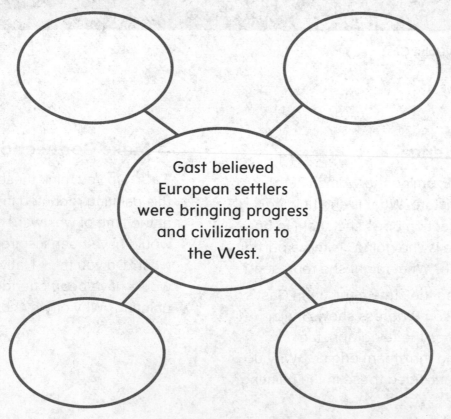

Gast believed European settlers were bringing progress and civilization to the West.

Investigate!

Read pages 366–377 in your Research Companion. Use your investigative skills to determine the point of view of a person or group of people from the lesson. Use the organizer to track key details that support this point of view.

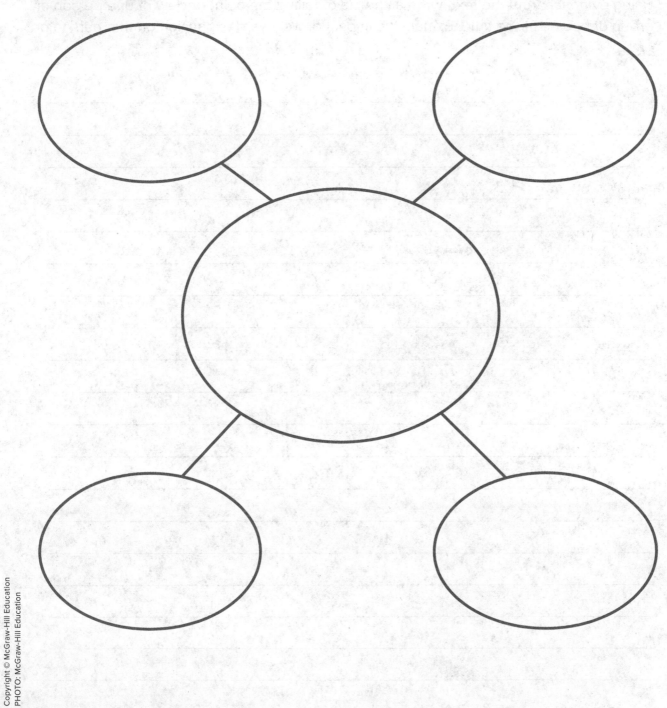

Think About It

What were some positive and negative effects of westward expansion?

Write About It

Write an Article

Using evidence from the text, write an article detailing the point of view of one person or group of people at the time. Explain the impact of westward expansion on that person or group.

_____

_____

_____

_____

_____

_____

_____

_____

_____

_____

_____

_____

_____

_____

_____

_____

Talk About It

Share Your Article

Work with a partner who wrote about a person or group different from yours. How did the views and actions of these people impact one another?

Connect to the

History

Pull It Together

How is the Indian Removal Act in conflict with the spirit in which the United States was founded? What does the Indian Removal Act reveal about the character of the nation at that time?

_____

_____

_____

_____

_____

_____

_____

_____

Inquiry Project Notes

_____

_____

_____

_____

_____

What Conflicts and Compromises Shaped the North and South?

Lesson Outcomes

What Am I Learning?

In this lesson, you're going to use your investigative skills to explore the conflicts and compromises that shaped the North and South.

Why Am I Learning It?

Reading and talking about the conflicts and compromises that shaped the North and South will help you understand why the United States had a civil war.

How Will I Know That I Learned It?

You will be able to explain how conflicts and compromises between the North and South led to the Civil War.

Talk About It

Look Examine the picture. What are the views of the person who made this flyer? How do you know?

NOTICE.

THE DUTCHESS COUNTY

ANTI-SLAVERY
SOCIETY

Will hold its first Annual Meeting at the house of Stephen E. Flagler, in the village of *Pleasant Valley*,

ON THURSDAY,
The 25th inst.

☞Several gentlemen will ADDRESS the meeting.☜

A neat and spacious Room, fitted for a large audience of Ladies and Gentlemen, is provided for the occasion.

All who feel an interest in the PRESERVATION OF THEIR LIBERTIES are respectfully invited to attend.

P. S. Meeting for Business at 11, A. M.—for Addresses at half past 2, P. M.

April 22, 1839.

An announcement for an anti-slavery meeting

1 Inspect

Read

Examine the primary source. What kind of document is it?

Circle words in the primary source that appear to be words for law and politics.

Underline important details in the introductory text such as:

- Who is involved in this case?
- What was the decision?
- Why is it important?

My Notes

_____

_____

_____

_____

_____

_____

_____

_____

_____

_____

_____

The Dred Scott Decision

The case of *Dred Scott* v. *John F. A. Sandford* is widely considered the worst decision the Supreme Court of the United States has ever made. Dred Scott was born into slavery and purchased by Dr. John Emerson in Missouri. Emerson later moved to Illinois and then the Wisconsin territory. Both of these places were free states. Emerson and Scott then returned to Missouri, where Emerson died. Scott tried to buy his freedom from Emerson's widow, but she refused. Antislavery lawyers helped Scott file a lawsuit. They argued that Scott should have been freed as soon as he had entered a free state. Initially, the state court sided with Scott and said he was free. The Missouri Supreme Court reversed the decision. At one point, Emerson's widow transferred ownership of Scott to her brother, John F.A. Sanford (misspelled in court documents) and a new lawsuit was brought against him. The case finally reached the U.S. Supreme Court. Chief Justice Roger Brooke Taney declared that African Americans were not American citizens and could not file a lawsuit. Furthermore, he claimed that the Missouri Compromise was unconstitutional and that slavery could not be restricted in any territory.

Dred Scott

In Their Words...

Chief Justice Roger Taney

5. When the Constitution was adopted, [African Americans] were not regarded in any of the States as members of the community which constituted the State, and were not numbered among its "people or citizen." Consequently, the special rights and immunities guaranteed to citizens do not apply to them. And not being "citizens" within the meaning of the Constitution, they are not entitled to sue in that character in a court of the United States, and the Circuit Court has not jurisdiction in such a suit.

. . .

9. The change in public opinion and feeling in relation to the African race, which has taken place since the adoption of the Constitution, cannot change its construction and meaning, and it must be construed and administered now according to its true meaning and intention when it was formed and adopted.

—from *Dred Scott v. John F. A. Sanford*, majority opinion of Chief Justice Taney

2 Find Evidence

Reread Summarize the excerpts from the opinion of Chief Justice Taney.

Think What was Taney's view of African Americans?

3 Make Connections

What arguments could be made against Taney's opinion?

Explore Problem and Solution

Text is often organized by presenting problems and then showing how those problems have been or could be solved.

1. **Read the text once all the way through.**

   This will tell you what the text is about.

2. **Look at the section titles to see how the text is organized.**

   This will help you find key events, decisions, and policies in the text.

3. **Find specific problems.**

   While reading, ask yourself what problems people in the early United States had.

4. **Look for specific solutions.**

   While reading, also ask yourself which particular laws, decisions, or compromises offered solutions to those problems.

COLLABORATE

Based on the text you read, work with your class to determine the solution to the problem of Dred Scott's legal status. Complete the chart below.

Problem	Solution
Dred Scott sued for his freedom.	

Investigate!

Read pages 378–387 in your Research Companion. Use your investigative skills to look for text evidence that tells you what conflicts the North and South had and how people attempted to solve them. This chart will help you organize your notes.

Problem	Solution
The country wants to maintain an equal number of free and slave states as they gain new territory.	
	The government creates tariffs.
Abolitionists need to convince people slavery is wrong.	
California citizens want it to be a free state.	
	Border ruffians enter Kansas to affect the vote.

Think About It

Review your research. Based on the information you have gathered, how successful were the compromises designed to keep the country together?

Write About It

Write a Letter Choose one of the compromises or solutions that you learned about in this chapter. Write a letter to a legislator saying what you think about the compromise or solution, and then give suggestions on how it might be improved.

_____

_____

_____

_____

_____

_____

_____

_____

_____

_____

_____

_____

_____

_____

_____

_____

Talk About It

Defend Your Claim Share your letter with a partner. Analyze each other's letters and look for possible problems. Suggest ways to improve your solutions.

Connect to the **EQ**

ESSENTIAL QUESTION

Pull It Together

Was the Civil War unavoidable? Think about the differences between the North and South and the attempts to settle conflicts with compromises and laws. Use text evidence to support your opinion.

_____

_____

_____

_____

_____

_____

_____

_____

_____

_____

_____

ESSENTIAL EQ QUESTION

What Do the Early Years of the United States Reveal About the Character of the Nation?

Inquiry Project

Create a Museum Gallery

Remember, for this project you will create a gallery of paintings that depict the United States during its early years and write a museum card for each painting describing it.

Complete Your Project

Use the checklist below to evaluate your project. If you left anything out, now's your chance to fix it!

☐ Conduct research to find three paintings that depict the early years of the nation.

☐ For each painting, research its artist, the year it was painted, and its meaning or significance.

☐ Consider how your chosen paintings tell a story about the character and spirit of the United States.

☐ Create a museum card for each painting from your research.

Share Your Project

Now it's time to present your museum gallery to the class. Present each painting and its card to the class. Explain why you chose each painting as you tell about its story. Describe to your classmates how your paintings tell a story about the character and spirit of the United States.

Reflect on Your Project

Think about the work you did in this chapter and on your project. Use the questions below to help guide your thoughts.

1. Why did you choose your three paintings? _____

_____

2. How did you conduct your research? Is there anything you

would do differently next time? _____

_____

3. How did you make sure that your sources were reliable? _____

_____

Chapter Connections

Use pictures, words, or both to reflect on what you learned in this chapter.

The most interesting thing I learned:

Something I learned from a classmate:

A connection I can make with my own life:

Trail of Tears

Original Route

How Do Economics And Finances Affect
People's Decisions?

Money Is the Root of All Travel

The early days of the nation were full of decisions both for the government and the people living in the United States. Many of these decisions involved moving to new places. People immigrated to the United States. People moved westward within the United States. These decisions were influenced by economic forces. These same economic forces continue to influence people's decisions today. Let's look at how economic forces affect the decisions that people make about their careers, where they live, and how they live.

This woman has a job designing building plans at an architectural office. Different jobs require different skills and types of knowledge.

Talk About It
COLLABORATE

Discuss Jobs

Look at the job in the image. What qualities do you think this job requires? What job would you like to do in the future? What qualities do you already have that make you a good fit for the job, and what knowledge or skills do you still need to learn?

Investigate!

Read about economics and finances on pages 394–399 in your Research Companion. As you read, think about the question: **How Do Economics and Finances Affect People's Decisions?**

Think About It

Take a Stand

Think about the economic choices people make every day. How are choices like buying food or gasoline for a car different from a choice to buy a ticket to see a movie?

Write About It

Write and Cite Evidence

In the "Expense" column, list things you might spend money on in a month. Decide what you need to spend money on and what you do not need to spend money on. If you have decided that some things are not necessary, you might have money left over. Weigh the costs and benefits of buying something you want now versus saving that money for later.

Expense	Cost ($)	Necessary?

Spending vs. Saving:

_____

_____

Talk About It

Defend Your Claim

Explain to a partner why you chose to buy something you wanted at the end of the month or why you chose to save your money. Discuss the costs and benefits of both choices.

THE CALIFORNIA GOLD RUSH

CHARACTERS

Narrator

Susanna Jones
(owner of a general store)

Louisa Lansdown *(sister of Joe)*

Malcolm Roberts *(husband of Lily)*

Joe Lansdown *(brother of Louisa)*

Martin Baker

Lily Roberts *(wife of Malcolm)*

Narrator: In December 1848, President James K. Polk announced that gold had been found in the California hills. Soon thousands of people traveled west to mine for gold. They dreamed of striking it rich. These men and women became known as the Forty-niners because many made their journey in 1849.

Louisa and Joe Lansdown are Forty-niners. They have just arrived in California. The young brother and sister head to a general store for supplies.

(Susanna *arranges goods on the store counter.* Louisa *and* Joe *burst through the door.*)

Joe: Excuse me, ma'am; my sister and I would like to buy some supplies.

Susanna: Where are you folks from?

Joe: Maryland. We came by wagon. It took months!

Louisa: We're going to get rich. I can't wait to start digging for gold!

Susanna: I'll show you a few things that every miner needs.

(Martin *enters with a hand pressed to his back.*)

Martin: Oh my aching back!

Susanna: Don't pay any attention to him. He's always complaining!

Martin: Before I left home, I figured it would be a year of pain for a lifetime of riches. Well, I guess I got the pain part!

Joe: And you got rich too, right?

Martin: HA! All I got was backbreaking labor. Ten hours a day, knee-deep in ice-cold water: digging, sifting, washing. Panning dirt just to find more dirt! Never so much as a twinkling lump of rock, much less gold.

Susanna: People are coming from all around the world to strike it rich. I've seen folks from Mexico, Ireland, Germany, France—even Turkey!

Martin: Every day there are more miners and less and less gold.

Susanna: (Susanna *is starting to worry about making a sale. She tries to be positive.*) So you'll need good tools! I have a shovel that will dig through just about anything. Take a look.

Louisa: Wait a minute. Are you saying that you didn't find *any* gold, sir?

Martin: Young lady, do I look like a wealthy man? Ow!

Susanna: Now back to those supplies. I can give you a great deal on this pan — only twenty dollars!

Joe: Twenty dollars! That's half our savings!

Susanna: Blame it on Sam Billington, the wealthiest man in California!

Just before the Gold Rush, he bought every pickax, pan, and shovel for miles around. By the time Forty-niners like you arrived, Sam Billington was sitting on his own gold mine. Can't mine without tools, right?

Martin: There's always someone looking to separate a hardworking man from his money.

(Malcolm *enters, holding an empty bottle, limping a little bit.*)

Malcolm: Susanna! You have any more of that lotion?

Susanna: Sure. I'll be right back.

(She leaves the room to look in the storage closet.)

Louisa: What kind of lotion is it?

Malcolm: It's a gold-attracting lotion. All you have to do it spread it around on your clothes, climb to the top of a mountain, and roll down. By the time you get to the bottom, you'll have enough gold dust stuck to you to live happily ever after.

Joe: That sounds pretty dangerous. And hey, if the lotion makes you rich, why do you have to buy more?

Malcolm: Nah, it don't hurt too bad. And the bottle says that it can take a few tries. But for only ten dollars a bottle, it's worth it. You ought to give it a try.

(Susanna *returns holding a bottle.*)

Susanna: Here we are, Malcolm. Ten dollars.

(Malcolm *reaches into his pocket but, before he can hand over the money,* Lily *storms into the store.*)

Lily: Malcolm Roberts, don't you dare spend my money on your foolishness!

(Malcolm *turns to face her.*)

Malcolm: Aw but Lily, it could make us rich!

Lily: Rich? The only way you'll ever see money is if I earn it with my housework.

Louisa: Can you really earn money by doing housework?

Lily: You'd be surprised how much money a woman can make here. Why, a hardworking woman can make more money in California than most men!

Louisa: What do you mean?

Lily: Well, gold is in short supply. That's what makes it valuable. A woman who knows how to cook, clean, and mend clothes is almost as rare as that gold! She can charge just about as much as she likes.

Joe: Well, Louisa, it looks like you can make money, at least!

Louisa: You're just jealous because I know how to cook, clean, mend clothes, AND mine for gold!

Susanna: Let's get back to business. You're going to need a pan if you're going to mine. I've got one in copper if you're interested.

(Susanna *continues to show her merchandise to* Louisa *and* Joe, *who seem much less interested.*)

Narrator: If Louisa and Joe were like most Forty-niners, they did not strike gold and get rich. Most people who grew wealthy during the Gold Rush made their money by selling supplies, not by finding gold.

Many Forty-niners stayed in California after the Gold Rush ended. They came from so many different places that they gave California a diverse, adventurous, and hard-working population.

Write About It

Write a play about Louisa and Joe two months after their arrival in California. Set the play in Susanna Jones's general store. What do you predict will have happened to Louisa and Joe in two months?

Chapter 8

The Civil War and Reconstruction

ESSENTIAL EQ QUESTION

What Was the Effect of the Civil War on U.S. Society?

In this chapter, you will read about how the Civil War broke out and was fought, and how the country came back together again. You will explore the strategies of each side and how certain battles led to the conclusion of the war. You will discover people who played key roles before, during, and after the war. Your investigations will help you answer the Essential Question, and the Inquiry Project will provide a chance to gather your research together.

Talk About It COLLABORATE

With a partner, discuss questions you have about how the Civil War affected U.S. society. As you read and research, look for answers to any questions you have. Let's get started!

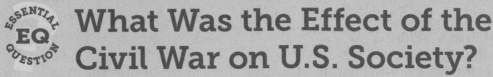

Inquiry Project

The Civil War and Reconstruction News Show

In this project, you will work with a team to prepare and produce a 10-minute news show about the Civil War and Reconstruction. Model your segments on a TV news show. Include fictional interviews with people who lived at the time. Present your news show as a play if recording is not possible.

Project Checklist

☐ **List** important events, people, and ideas.

☐ **Assign** people different parts of the task, such as writing, directing, reporting, acting, designing graphics, and recording.

☐ **Write** scripts for reporters and interviews.

☐ **Prepare** visuals, such as photos and illustrations.

☐ **Rehearse** the performance before filming it or presenting it to the class.

My Research Plan

Write down any research questions you have that will help you plan your project. You can add questions as you carry out your research.

_____

_____

_____

_____

_____

_____

casualties   My Notes

☐ Know It!   _____

☐ Heard It!   _____

☐ Don't Know It!

_____

draft   My Notes

☐ Know It!   _____

☐ Heard It!   _____

☐ Don't Know It!

_____

enlist   My Notes

☐ Know It!   _____

☐ Heard It!   _____

☐ Don't Know It!

_____

ironclads   My Notes

☐ Know It!   _____

☐ Heard It!   _____

☐ Don't Know It!

_____

pardon   My Notes

☐ Know It!   _____

☐ Heard It!   _____

☐ Don't Know It!

_____

popular sovereignty

☐ Know It!
☐ Heard It!
☐ Don't Know It!

My Notes

_____

_____

_____

secede

☐ Know It!
☐ Heard It!
☐ Don't Know It!

My Notes

_____

_____

_____

sharecropping

☐ Know It!
☐ Heard It!
☐ Don't Know It!

My Notes

_____

_____

_____

siege

☐ Know It!
☐ Heard It!
☐ Don't Know It!

My Notes

_____

_____

_____

strategy

☐ Know It!
☐ Heard It!
☐ Don't Know It!

My Notes

_____

_____

_____

Lesson Outcomes

What Am I Learning?

In this lesson, you're going to use your investigative skills to explore the events that led to the start of the Civil War.

Why Am I Learning It?

Reading and talking about these events will help you understand the causes and effects of the Civil War.

How Will I Know That I Learned It?

You will be able to identify the chronology of events that led to the Civil War, state an opinion about which event was most important, and support your opinion with evidence.

Talk About It

COLLABORATE

Look at the Details Examine the image and read the caption. What do you think is happening here? What challenges do you think there were to attacking Fort Sumter?

Bombardment of Fort Sumter, Charleston Harbor by Currier and Ives

Copyright © McGraw-Hill Education
PHOTO: South Carolina Convention. Declaration of the Immediate Cause Which Induce and Justify the Secession of South Carolina from the Federal Union. Charleston: Evans & Cogswell, 1860.

1 Inspect

Read Look at the text. What is the purpose of this text?

- **Circle** words you don't know.
- **Underline** clues that help you understand unfamiliar words and concepts.
- **Discuss** with a partner the reasons the authors give to explain their decision to leave the Union.

My Notes

_____

_____

_____

_____

_____

_____

_____

_____

_____

_____

South Carolina Responds

Southern states worried that the 1860 presidential election would affect their rights. After Abraham Lincoln was elected, South Carolina became the first state to **secede**, or withdraw, from the Union. The *Declaration of the Immediate Causes Which Induce and Justify the Secession of South Carolina from the Federal Union* states the reasons behind the state's decision.

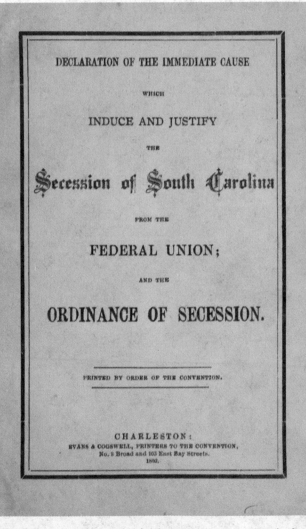

South Carolina issued this document and seceded from the Union in December 1860.

PRIMARY SOURCE

In Their Words... The state government of South Carolina

A geographical line has been drawn across the Union, and all the States north of that line have united in the election of a man to the high office of President of the United States, whose opinions and purposes are hostile to slavery. . . .

On the 4th day of March next, this party will take possession of the Government. It has announced that the South shall be excluded from the common territory, that the judicial tribunals shall be made sectional, and that a war must be waged against slavery until it shall cease throughout the United States.

The guaranties of the Constitution will then no longer exist; the equal rights of the States will be lost. The slaveholding States will no longer have the power of self-government, or self-protection, and the Federal Government will have become their enemy.

—from *Declaration of the Immediate Causes Which Induce and Justify the Secession of South Carolina from the Federal Union*

2 Find Evidence

Reread Reread the text from South Carolina's declaration of secession. What is the attitude of the South Carolina government toward Abraham Lincoln? Cite details to support your answer.

3 Make Connections

Write Summarize South Carolina's key concerns for the Union after the election.

Explore Cause and Effect

Many events you will read about in this chapter have a cause-and-effect relationship. A **cause** is an event that makes something else happen. An **effect** is an event that happens as a result of the cause. Looking for cause-and-effect relationships can help you better understand what you read.

1. Read the text all the way through.

This will help you understand the main ideas in the text.

2. Pay attention to chronology.

Often, texts present cause-and-effect relationships in the order that events happened. Look for years. Note which events happen first, next, and last.

3. Look for related events.

As you read, ask yourself, *What happened, and why?* The answers to these questions will help you identify causes and effects.

4. Remember that an event may have more than one cause and effect.

Keep in mind that cause-and-effect relationships can be complex. Often, an event will have more than one cause and more than one effect.

 Based on the text you read, work with your class to
COLLABORATE complete the chart below.

Cause		Effect
Abraham Lincoln won the election of 1860.	⟶	

Investigate!

Read pages 408–419 in your Research Companion. Use your investigative skills to find cause-and-effect relationships in the text. Look for events in the text that led to the Civil War. To complete the graphic organizer, list each event as a "cause." Write what happened as a result of each event as an "effect."

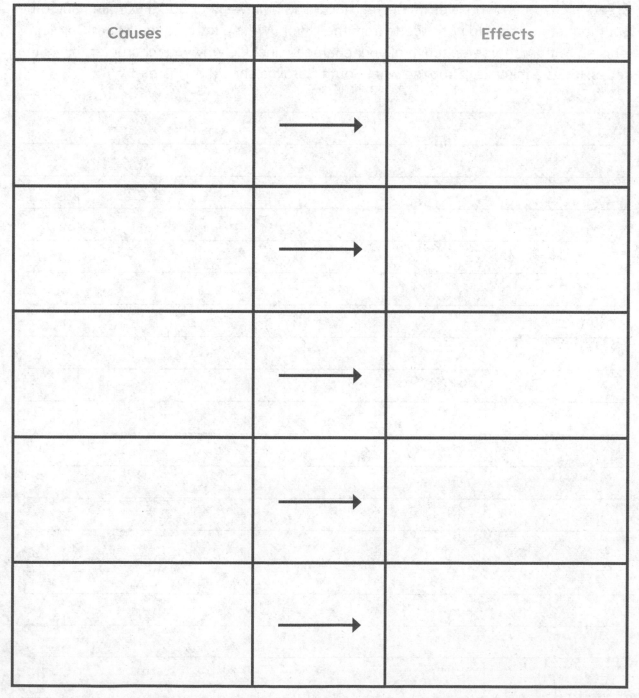

Causes		Effects
	→	
	→	
	→	
	→	
	→	

Think About It

Review your research. Based on the information you have gathered, could secession have been avoided? If so, how?

Write About It

Write a Letter

Create a character who lives in the year 1860 and believes that South Carolina and other Southern states should not secede from the Union. Write a letter to the South Carolina legislature from the perspective of your character. Include why your character thinks that secession is a mistake. Propose what South Carolina should do instead.

Talk About It

Share Your Letter Work with a partner. Take turns reading your letters to each other. Explain who your character is to help your partner understand the character's perspective about secession. Do the details in each letter help communicate the characters' perspectives? Are there details that could be included to clarify why each character thinks secession is a mistake?

History

Connect to the

Make Connections

Think about what you have learned about the causes of the Civil War. What do they have in common with the American Revolution? How are the different?

_____

_____

_____

_____

_____

Inquiry Project Notes

_____

_____

_____

_____

_____

_____

_____

Lesson Outcomes

What Am I Learning?

In this lesson, you are going to use your investigative skills to determine the strengths each side brought to the Civil War.

Why Am I Learning It?

Reading and talking about the Union and the Confederacy will help you understand their strengths and the challenges they faced.

How Will I Know That I Learned It?

You will be able to compare and contrast the strategies each side tried to use to win the war, and you will write an editorial that summarizes one of the strategies.

Talk About It

COLLABORATE

Look at the Photo Why would soldiers have portraits taken before they left for war?

Portrait of a Civil War soldier

1 Inspect

Read Think about the title and skim the text. What do you think this text will be about?

- **Circle** words you don't know.
- **Underline** clues that tell you the advantages ironclads had over wooden ships.
- **Discuss** with a partner why both sides wanted ironclads.

My Notes

_____

_____

_____

_____

_____

_____

_____

_____

_____

_____

_____

Ironclad Ships

Gunboats were essential military weapons when the Civil War began. Navies used these small, fast ships in rivers and along coasts to shoot at targets on the shore. Traditional gunboats were wooden. The gunboats needed to withstand hits from bullets and cannonballs, so navies began to build ships that were covered in iron—the **ironclads**. To construct an ironclad, shipbuilders laid sheets of iron over a wooden frame. Navies often used old wooden ships for the frames.

An ironclad gunboat had to ride high in the water so it could easily enter and protect shallow harbors. Many designs were used. Some Union ironclads had a round, rotating gun turret. This made it easier for the ship to fight in open water, where the targets were other ships. The Confederacy designed ships with sloping metal sides.

The Confederate navy converted an old steamship called the *Merrimack* into an ironclad and renamed it the *Virginia*. The *Virginia* sank two Union ships and damaged many more. It famously fought a Union ironclad called the *Monitor*.

PRIMARY SOURCE

In Their Words... Samuel Lewis, alias Peter Truskitt, describing the Union *Monitor*:

She was a little bit the strangest craft I had ever seen, nothing but a few inches of deck above the water line, her big round tower in the center, and the pilothouse at the end . . . We had confidence in her though, from the start, for the little ship looked somehow like she meant business, and it didn't take us long to learn the ropes.

—from *Camp and Field: Sketches of Army Life Written by Those who Followed the Flag. '61-'65*

Ironclad ships were used by both sides during the Civil War.

2 Find Evidence

Reread How does the article help you understand the similarities and differences among ships in the Civil War?

Examine Reread details that show how ships differed.

3 Make Connections

Talk Why did navies build ironclad ships? What are the strengths of the different designs?

Explore Compare and Contrast

The Union and the Confederacy both used ironclad ships, but the designs were different. When you **compare**, you identify how two or more items in a category, such as people, events, or ironclad ships, are the same. When you **contrast**, you identify how two or more items in a category are different.

To compare and contrast:

1. **Identify features that the items have in common.**

   Record the similarities, and think about why the items share these features.

2. **Identify how the items are different.**

   Record the differences and think about why the items are different.

3. **Draw conclusions about the similarities and differences.**

   Ask yourself, what do these similarities and differences add to my understanding?

Depending on the items you compare and contrast, there may be many more similarities than differences or many more differences than similarities.

 Based on the text you have just read, work with your class to complete the organizer below.

	Union and Confederate Similarities	Union and Confederate Differences
Ironclad Ships	Iron armor protected ships from gunfire.	

Investigate!

Read pages 420–429 in your Research Companion. Use your investigative skills to look for text evidence of similarities and differences between the Union and the Confederacy. This diagram will help you organize your notes. There may not be an answer for every box.

	Union and Confederate Similarities	Union and Confederate Differences
Population		
Expectations		
Strategies		
Resources		

Think About It

Review your research. Based on your research, which side had the essential strengths for winning the war?

Write About It

Editorial Imagine you are a Union general from the North or a Confederate general from the South. Write a short newspaper editorial explaining why you believe your side will win the war. Make sure to explain how your strategy for winning the war will overcome the strengths of the opposing side.

_____

_____

_____

_____

_____

_____

_____

_____

_____

_____

_____

_____

_____

_____

Talk About It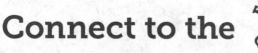

Discuss Compare editorials and opinions in a small group. Together, discuss why each side thought it could win.

Geography

Connect to the

Pull It Together

Write and Cite Evidence Early in the war, which side had the better strategy? In other words, which side was in the better position to win? Why? Support your opinion with evidence.

_____

_____

_____

_____

_____

_____

_____

_____

_____

_____

_____

 Inquiry Project Notes

_____

_____

_____

What Was It Like to Live During the Civil War?

Lesson Outcomes

What Am I Learning?

In this lesson, you're going to use your investigative skills to learn how the Civil War affected the lives of people who lived in the United States at that time.

Why Am I Learning It?

Reading and talking about how people lived during the Civil War will help you learn more about the changes that took place and how those changes affected the country.

How Will I Know That I Learned It?

You will be able to explain how and why the Civil War affected various groups of people differently.

Talk About It

COLLABORATE

Look at the Details The picture on page 323 is of Rose O'Neal Greenhow, a Confederate spy. Does she look like a spy to you? Why or why not?

Letter written in code by Rose Greenhow

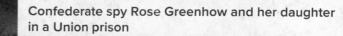

Confederate spy Rose Greenhow and her daughter in a Union prison

1 Inspect

Read Look at the text. Look at the title. What will the text be about?

- **Circle** words you don't know.
- **Underline** clues that help you understand unfamiliar words and concepts.
- **Discuss** with a partner the roles that boys and young men played in the Civil War.

My Notes

_____

_____

_____

_____

_____

_____

_____

_____

_____

_____

_____

_____

The Youngest People on the Battlefield

Many boys and young men were just as eager as their older relatives and neighbors to enlist. Soldiers had to be 18 years old, but musicians, such as drummer boys, could legally join at the age of 16. Some lied about their age so they could join the Union or Confederate armies early. Johnny Clem was one such boy. Clem ran away from home at the age of 9 to join the Union army. Too young and small for his age, he did not fool the Union officials who enlisted his father and brother. He tried again, and when the second regiment turned him away, he refused to go home until they changed their minds. Clem took an unofficial position as a drummer boy and stayed with the Army. At the age of 12, he was promoted to sergeant and became the youngest person to fight in the Civil War. Although he was wounded several times and eventually captured, Clem thrived in the chaos of the battlefield. Other drummer boys and young soldiers had different experiences.

Johnny Clem served in the Union Army as a young boy.

In Their Words... Charles W. Bardeen, a 15-year-old drummer

. . . I was certainly scared. One shell had exploded near enough so that I could realize its effects, and the one thing I wanted was to get where no more shells could burst around me. This patriotic hero who had declared in front of campfires how he had longed for gore would have liked to be tucked up once more in his little trundle bed.

—from *A Little Fifer's War Diary*

2 Find Evidence

Reread Both Johnny Clem and Charles W. Bardeen were drummer boys. How were their experiences alike and different? Cite details to support your answer.

3 Make Connections

Talk Why do you think the Union and Confederate Armies had an age requirement?

COLLABORATE

Explore Main Idea and Details

The **main idea** of a text is its most important idea. This is what authors want readers to learn about the topic. **Key details** are facts, examples, and other evidence that develop and support the main idea. Sometimes authors clearly state the main idea in a text, but sometimes readers need to use details to infer the main idea.

To find the main idea and key details:

1. **Read the text all the way through.**

   This will help you determine what the text is about.

2. **Look at section titles.**

   These are clues that tell you what each section is about. Putting these clues together will help you identify the main idea of the whole text.

3. **Look for key details.**

   Look for important facts, examples, and other evidence the author includes.

4. **Think about connections.**

   Ask yourself, How do these details help develop or support the main idea?

 Based on the text you read, work with your class to complete the chart below.

Detail
Detail
Boys and young men responded to the war in different ways. Main Idea

Investigate!

Read pages 430–441 in your Research Companion. Use your investigative skills to look for text evidence that tells you key details and the main idea. Use this chart to track details and determine the main idea of the lesson. Think about the challenges faced by soldiers and civilians during the Civil War.

Details
Details
Details
Details
Details
Main Idea

Think About It

Review your research. Based on the information you have gathered, how did the Civil War affect Americans?

Write About It

Write a Letter

Create a character who lives during the Civil War. It may be a draftee, a woman, an African American, a young drummer boy, or someone else. First, decide the character details. Where does the character live? What are his or her feelings about the war? Next, write a letter that tells the character's perspective on the war. Include details from your research.

_____

_____

_____

_____

_____

_____

_____

_____

_____

_____

_____

_____

_____

_____

_____

_____

Talk About It

Share Your Thinking Find a partner who chose to write from the perspective of a different character. Share your letters. Take turns discussing your character's perspective of the war and the details you chose to support it.

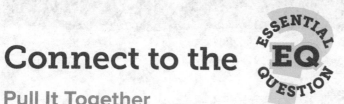

Connect to the

History

Pull It Together

Think about what you have learned about how people lived during the Civil War. What positive and negative effects did the Civil War have on Americans?

_____

_____

_____

_____

_____

_____

_____

_____

_____

_____

_____

Inquiry Project Notes

_____

_____

_____

_____

Lesson 4

How Did Key Moments Lead to the End of the Civil War?

Lesson Outcomes

What Am I Learning?

In this lesson, you're going to use your investigative skills to explore what battles and other events caused the Union to win the Civil War.

Why Am I Learning It?

Reading and talking about the key moments that ended the Civil War will help you understand the important effects the war had on U.S. history.

How Will I Know That I Learned It?

You will be able to explain why the North won the Civil War and preserved the Union.

Talk About It

COLLABORATE

Look at the Details How would you feel if you visited this place? Why might Civil War cannons and monuments have been placed there?

The stone monuments at Gettysburg National Military Park honor the regiments that fought in the battle.

1 Inspect

Read Look at the title. What do you think this text will be about?

- **Circle** words you don't know.
- **Underline** clues that tell you:
  - Why did Abraham Lincoln give this speech?
  - When did he give the speech?
  - What important ideas did Lincoln want to talk about?

My Notes

_____

_____

_____

_____

_____

_____

_____

_____

_____

_____

_____

_____

A Speech for the Ages

Abraham Lincoln's Gettysburg Address is one of the most famous speeches in the history of the United States. For many years, schoolchildren were expected to learn this speech and be able to recite it from memory. Although the Gettysburg Address was intended to dedicate a new cemetery at a major battlefield in 1863, Lincoln used his speech to address even greater issues. He wanted to tell Americans why the soldiers who died at Gettysburg were heroes and why it was important to continue fighting the Civil War.

In the first line of the address, the word *score* means "twenty."

Lincoln's Gettysburg Address lasted about three minutes. His respectful audience interrupted the speech five times with applause.

PRIMARY SOURCE

In Their Words... Abraham Lincoln

Four score and seven years ago our fathers brought forth, upon this continent, a new nation, conceived in Liberty, and dedicated to the proposition that all men are created equal.

Now we are engaged in a great civil war, testing whether that nation, or any nation, so conceived, and so dedicated, can long endure. We are met here on a great battlefield of that war. We have come to dedicate a portion of it as a final resting place for those who here gave their lives that that nation might live. It is altogether fitting and proper that we should do this.

But in a larger sense we can not dedicate—we can not consecrate—we can not hallow this ground. The brave men, living and dead, who struggled, here, have consecrated it far above our poor power to add or detract. The world will little note, nor long remember, what we say here, but can never forget what they did here. It is for us, the living, rather to be dedicated to the unfinished work which they have, thus far, so nobly carried on. It is rather for us to be here dedicated to the great task remaining before us—that from these honored dead we take increased devotion to that cause for which they here gave the last full measure of devotion—that we here highly resolve that these dead shall not have died in vain; that this nation shall have a new birth of freedom; and that this government of the people, by the people, for the people, shall not perish from the earth.

—The Gettysburg Address

2 Find Evidence

Reread What key ideas from U.S. history does Lincoln mention? How are these ideas connected with the events he is discussing?

What is Lincoln afraid will happen if he does not succeed in the "great task"?

3 Make Connections

Talk What event is Lincoln talking about in the first sentence of his speech? How does he connect this event with the main topic of his speech?

Explore Chronology

Thinking about chronology, or the order in which things happen, will help you make connections between related events.

1. **Read the text all the way through.**

   This will help you understand how the text is organized.

2. **Look for verbs.**

   The verbs will help show what events the text is about.

3. **Look for transition words that indicate a shift in time.**

   Words such as *then, later,* or *after* can show that the writer is starting to discuss a different event.

4. **Find key facts about each event.**

   As you read about each event, think about what the key facts and details suggest about which events were important in the Civil War.

 Based on the text you read, work with your class to complete the chart below.

Date	Event	Key Facts
	Gettysburg Address	

Investigate!

Read pages 442–453 in your Research Companion. Use your investigative skills to look for text evidence that tells you which events led to the end of the Civil War. Fill in the chart below with information about the events.

Year	Event	Key Facts

Think About It

Review your research. Based on the information you have gathered, which events do you think led to the end of the Civil War?

Write About It

Take a Stand

Write and Cite Evidence Write an opinion essay about which event was most important in leading to the end of the Civil War. Why was this event more important than other events? Use facts and details from the text to support your opinion.

_____

_____

_____

_____

_____

_____

_____

_____

_____

_____

_____

_____

_____

_____

Talk About It

Defend Your Claim

Share your response with a partner. Discuss the event you chose as most important. Which evidence best supports your claims?

History

Connect to the

Pull It Together Which side had the essential strengths for winning the war? How are these strengths related to the event you chose as most important in ending the war?

_____

_____

_____

_____

_____

_____

_____

_____

_____

_____

Inquiry Project Notes

_____

_____

_____

_____

What Challenges Did the United States Face After the Civil War?

Lesson Outcomes

What Am I Learning?

In this lesson, you're going to use your investigative skills to explore how the United States changed following the end of the Civil War.

Why Am I Learning It?

Reading and talking about the events that happened after the Civil War will help you understand how Reconstruction impacted the nation.

How Will I Know That I Learned It?

You will be able to show an understanding of the challenges Americans faced in the years following the Civil War.

Talk About It

COLLABORATE

Look Examine the picture and read the caption. What are the people doing? What do their actions suggest about their feelings for Abraham Lincoln?

President Lincoln's funeral procession in Washington, D.C., was a mile long.

Copyright © McGraw-Hill Education
TEXT: Lincoln, Abraham. "Second Inaugural Address." Washington, D.C., March 4, 1865. Library of Congress, Manuscript Division, Abraham Lincoln Papers: Series 3.

1 Inspect

Read Look at the text. Look at the title. What will the text be about?

- **Circle** words you don't know.
- **Underline** clues that help you understand unfamiliar words and concepts.
- **Discuss** with a partner the main points of Lincoln's address.

My Notes

_____

_____

_____

_____

_____

_____

_____

_____

_____

_____

_____

_____

_____

_____

_____

Lincoln's Second Inaugural Address

Toward the end of the Civil War, Abraham Lincoln was re-elected as president. When he was sworn in on March 4, 1865, he gave a speech called an inaugural address. The speech shown here is his second inaugural address, in which he talked about his hopes for the end of the war and the peace that would follow. Lincoln discussed the challenges of the war and looked for similarities among the Union and Confederate troops still fighting. He also referred to slavery as an "offense" that must come to an end. At the end of the speech, Lincoln expressed his hopes for rebuilding the nation after the war and his plan for a peaceful future.

PRIMARY SOURCE

In Their Words... Abraham Lincoln

Fondly do we hope—fervently do we pray—that this mighty scourge of war may speedily pass away. Yet, if God wills that it continue, until all the wealth piled by the bond-man's two hundred and fifty years of unrequited toil shall be sunk, and until every drop of blood drawn with the lash, shall be paid by another drawn with the sword, as was said three thousand years ago, so still it must be said "the judgments of the Lord, are true and righteous altogether."

With malice toward none; with charity for all; with firmness in the right, as God gives us to see the right, let us strive on to finish the work we are in; to bind up the nation's wounds; to care for him who shall have borne the battle, and for his widow, and his orphan to do all which may achieve and cherish a just, and a lasting peace, among ourselves, and with all nations.

—from Abraham Lincoln's second inaugural address, 1865

A handwritten copy of Lincoln's second inaugural address has been preserved by the Library of Congress.

2 Find Evidence

Reread What words tell you that Lincoln wanted to heal the nation and not punish the South? What specific words and phrases helped create that effect?

3 Make Connections

Talk What does this speech have in common with the Gettysburg Address?

COLLABORATE

Summarize

Summaries include only the most important information in a text. As you read, think about the most important ideas, facts, examples, and other evidence. Writing a summary helps you remember the main ideas and details in a text. It also helps you understand the text's structure.

1. **Read the text all the way through.**

   This will help you identify the main ideas in a text.

2. **Take notes.**

   As you reread, take notes on the most important people, places, events, and ideas. Remember to restate ideas in your own words and leave out your opinions.

3. **Follow the structure.**

   Summaries should reflect the same structure the author uses. If the text is written in chronological order, the events in your summary should be listed in the order in which they happened.

4. **Be concise.**

   Remember that summaries should be much shorter than the original text. Include only the most important ideas.

Based on the text you read, work with your class to complete the chart below.

Details	Lincoln talked about how hard the war was for both sides.		
Summary			

Investigate!

Read pages 454–463 in your Research Companion. Use your investigative skills to list important details and to write a summary of one section of the text.

Details				

Summary	

Think About It

Review your research. Based on the information you have gathered, how did Lincoln's death affect Reconstruction?

Write About It

Write and Cite Evidence How would Reconstruction have been different if Abraham Lincoln had lived? Include reasons and evidence to support your opinion.

_____

_____

_____

_____

_____

_____

_____

_____

_____

_____

_____

_____

_____

_____

_____

_____

_____

_____

Talk About It

Defend Your Claim Share your response with a partner. Take turns discussing your opinions and supporting evidence. Do you agree or disagree with your partner's opinion? Why?

History

Connect to the EQ

Pull It Together List the obstacles that were a challenge during Reconstruction and then state your opinion on the following question: What was the biggest problem during Reconstruction, and why?

_____

_____

_____

_____

_____

_____

_____

_____

_____

_____

Inquiry Project Notes

_____

_____

_____

_____

What Was the Effect of the Civil War on U.S. Society?

Inquiry Project

The Civil War and Reconstruction News Show

Remember that for this project you will work with a team to prepare and present a 10-minute news show about the Civil War and Reconstruction. Research important events and people from this era. Follow the format of a news program, including interviews. Make sure every person on your team has an assigned role. Practice your program before recording or presenting it to your class.

Complete Your Project

Use the checklist below to evaluate your project. If you left anything out, now's your chance to fix it!

☐ Perform the interviews you have written.

☐ Use visual displays to help develop key ideas.

☐ Provide a final statement that reviews the key ideas presented.

Share Your Project

When you present your news show to your class, be sure to rehearse your presentation. Speak slowly and clearly so the audience understands what you say. Look your listeners in the eye. Practice using video equipment before the presentation.

Reflect on Your Project

Think about your work in this chapter and on your project. Use the questions below to help guide your thoughts.

1. Why did you chose to include these events, people, and ideas of the Civil War and Reconstruction? _____

_____

2. How did you conduct your research? Is there anything you would do differently next time? _____

_____

3. How did you assign roles to each team member? _____

_____

Chapter Connections

Use pictures, words, or both to reflect on what you learned in this chapter.

The most interesting thing I learned:

Something I learned from a classmate:

A connection I can make with my own life:

How Have Young People in Modern Times Fought for a Better Life?

The IMPACT Today

Oftentimes, young people have taken a prominent role in civil rights movements. For example, in the spring of 1963, the Rev. Martin Luther King Jr. was in Birmingham, Alabama, to lead a protest against segregation. Dr. King and other civil rights leaders were having trouble getting enough adults to participate, so they asked children to join the protest. More than 600 were arrested and put in jail. The next day more than twice as many young people protested in Birmingham. The Birmingham police used attack dogs and fire hoses against the protesters. This upset people across the nation. Public opinion swung in favor of the protesters.

Young people protesting segregation during the Birmingham Children's March in 1963

Talk About It

Look at the Photograph

The photo shows African American children marching to express their desire for civil rights. What issues are important to you today?

Investigate!

Read about how young people have tried to make positive change on pages 466–471 of your Research Companion. As you read, think about the question: **How Have Young People in Modern Times Fought for a Better Life?**

Think About It

Take a Stand

Review your research. Based on the information you have gathered, which of the issues from the past are still issues today? How are these issues similar to and different from the way they were in the past?

Write About It

Write and Cite Evidence

Choose an issue that is important to you. How would you increase awareness of that issue? How could you make an impact today? List three ways you could increase people's awareness of your issue. Choose which way would be most effective, and explain why.

Issue That Is Important to You

_____

Ways You Could Raise Awareness

1. _____

   _____

2. _____

   _____

3. _____

   _____

Which way would be most effective? Why?

_____

_____

Talk About It

Defend Your Claim

Explain to a partner which method you chose for raising awareness of your issue. Discuss other methods for raising awareness.

Reference Source

The Reference Section has a glossary of vocabulary words from the chapters in this book. Use this section to explore new vocabulary as you investigate and take action.

Glossary

abolitionist a person who believed slavery was wrong and should be ended

amendment an addition to the Constitution

article a paragraph in a legal document

assembly a government legislature that represents the people of a particular place

B

bill a suggestion for a new law

blockade an obstacle preventing the movement of people or goods

boycott to refuse to do business or have contact with a person, group, company, country, or product

C

cash crop a plant that is grown for making money

casualties people killed or wounded during warfare

cede to give up something to someone else

charter a document granting someone ownership of something

claim to declare that a place belongs to one's country upon arrival at the place

colony a territory settled by people from another place, usually far away

commerce the buying and selling of goods

composition the way in which something is put together

conquest victory by an invading army

covenant a contract; an agreement

currency the type of money used in a particular place

delegate a person who represents other people

demand the level of need for something

dissension disagreement between members of a group over an important issue

diverse containing many types of people or things

draft a picking of persons for required military service

encomiendas system of forced labor in Spanish colonies

endeavor to try hard to achieve a goal

enlist to enroll for military service

environment the setting in which something takes place

fugitive a person who flees or has escaped

H

habitat an environment that is favorable to the survival of a species

harvest to take and gather such crops as wheat and corn for use

hieroglyph a type of ancient writing that uses pictures for words

hunter-gatherer an early human who lived by gathering wild plants and hunting animals

I

imposing putting in place by a government order

inflation increase in the cost of goods and services

interchangeable something that can be used in place of something else because it is identical

ironclads armored naval vessels

issue to give out or publish

J

jury a group of citizens that decides the outcome of a court case

L

loom a machine for making thread or yarn into cloth

M

Manifest Destiny the belief that it was divine will for the United States to expand westward to the Pacific Ocean

mercenary soldier from a different country who is paid to fight in a war

merchants people who buy and sell goods

mesa a flat-topped hill with steep sides

militia a group of citizens organized for military service

missionary person on a religious mission, usually to convert others to Christianity

monarch a king or queen who rules a nation

monopoly complete control of something

musket a long gun similar to a rifle

N

navigation the art of guiding a boat, plane, or other transportation vehicle

negotiate to discuss and bargain for a solution

O

oral history spoken records, including stories, that have been passed from one generation to the next

outpost a fort or other military structure established away from the main army to help guard against surprise attacks

P

pardon to excuse an offense without a penalty

physical relating to material objects; having actual form

policy an official position on an issue

popular sovereignty allowing people in each territory to decide on an issue themselves

potlatch a special feast given by Native Americans of the Northwest Coast, in which the guests receive gifts

prairie flat or gently rolling land covered mostly with grasses and wildflowers

press the news media, including newspapers and magazines, websites, and TV and radio

profiteer people who take advantage of a poor economic situation, hoarding goods and selling them at high prices to make a large profit

proprietor a person with the legal right or title to something

R

rebel person who defies authority

recession a temporary downturn in business activity

reconcile to become friendly again after a disagreement; to make peace with

reconciliation returning to the previous friendly condition of a relationship after a disagreement

repeal cancelation or withdrawal

resistance defense to diseases developed by the immune system

S

secede to withdraw

settlement town created by people in an area previously uninhabited by that people

sharecropping farming land for the owner in return for a share of the value of the crop

siege the placing of an army around a city to force it to surrender

slash-and-burn a method of clearing land for farming by cutting and burning trees

sovereign having independent authority

strategy a careful plan or method

surge sudden increase

term the period of during which an elected person is in office

totem pole a tall carved log used by Native Americans of the Northwest Coast to honor an important person or to mark a special event

traitor someone who betrays his or her country

unconstitutional an action or policy that goes against the Constitution of the United States

vandalism destruction of property

warship ship mounted with cannons or other large guns